Going It Alone

Sally Garratt

Gower

© Sally Garratt 1991

First published in hardback 1991 by Gower Publishing

Paperback edition published 1994 by
Gower Publishing
Gower House
Croft Road
Aldershot
Hants GU11 3HR
England

Gower
Old Post Road
Brookfield
Vermont 05036
USA

ISBN 0 566 7616 0

Printed and bound in Great Britain by
Hartnolls Ltd, Bodmin, Cornwall

Contents

Preface

Until I started on this book, I had not fully appreciated what it is I do as a consultant. Other books have been easier to write because they have been records of what I talk about nearly every day. This one is about what I *do* and how I do it, and that is much more difficult to describe. Putting the final touches to the manuscript at a friend's house in Provence makes me feel relieved that my part of the contract is nearly completed, apprehensive about what my peers will think of the content, and convinced that, as soon as I hand over the parcel to the publisher, I will think of all the points I meant to include and did not. All rather like a consultancy project, in fact!

Following my own advice about seeking the help of others if you yourself do not know the answers, I would like to thank sincerely the following people:

- So many fellow consultants, but particularly Roger Plant, John Teire, Janet McCallum and Krystyna Weinstein, for answering all my questions with good humour and understanding, and Sue Thame for allowing me to use her piece on p. xiv.
- Clients who have employed me over the years and friends in 'proper jobs', but particularly Diane Reeder (Roffey Park), Wendy Thorburn (Dun and Bradstreet), Dorothea Palmer Fry (Trebor), Keith Drinkwater (Children's Society), Terri Yuill (Housing Corporation), Barry Welch (British Telecom) and Derek Ashworth (Guinness) for taking the time to divulge what it is they look for in consultants.

- Ekke Anderle, for my chair.
- Bryan Gair, taxation adviser, who provided most of the answers in Chapter 5 and who has never shown anything more than mild disappointment when, yet again, the accounts are not ready on time!
- Susan Hay, now running her own nursery provision consultancy, for the Appendix on Professional Liability and Indemnity Insurance.
- Sandra Horn, clinical psychologist by training and long-standing friend by fate, for clarifying my thoughts on handling stress and relaxation.
- Margareta Hult, for Villa Gabrielle.
- James Konig, of C E Heath, who has managed our insurance portfolio since he was a mere lad and we were not much older.
- Clare Lorenz, for introducing me to the topic of 'Ethics' and for allowing me to work with her in her research into the subject, with particular reference to the professions.
- Suzie Morel, sometime tennis partner and teacher extraordinaire, who has helped me, through Alexander Technique and through her seemingly limitless range of skills and knowledge, to learn how to keep my unpredictable back in check and how to keep body, mind and spirit in balance.
- Malcolm Stern, of Gower, for asking me to write this book and for his support in bringing it to publication.
- and Bob Garratt: for writing the section on Intellectual Property and clarifying my thoughts on the Volume/Price/Cost equation; for helping me with the piece on choosing a car – a subject about which I have little knowledge and even less interest; for critically reviewing the manuscript as it evolved, and apparently not minding too much having his holiday in the sun interrupted by my interminable questions; and for being so unstintingly generous with time, advice and support, not just while this book was being written but always over the past twenty-seven years.

I have referred to my husband, Bob, often in the book. This is because we do work together, as well as individually, and it is to be expected that I should mention joint experiences. Our work is also, inevitably, something that we share, discuss and enjoy. If, therefore, I write 'we', I am not suffering from delusions of grandeur, just naturally embracing the two of us. Where Bob has the more appropriate examples to illustrate my points, I have used them – with his agreement, of course.

I have tried to avoid the clumsy 'his/her' or 'she/he'. Where the use of the singular pronoun is necessary, I have used only one, alternating between them in following chapters. I trust this will not offend anyone.

Most of what I have written is the result of experience and learning from my mistakes. Over the last twelve years, I have experienced mostly good times, and a few lows, but I would not change now – even if I could. As a headhunter told me a couple of years ago: 'You wouldn't get a job in an organization now – you'd be seen as too independent, too questioning, a potential troublemaker. Let's face it, you're unemployable!'

I am also very conscious of the generosity of others and have gratefully received advice from those wiser than me. I hope that one day, instead of being just clever, I, too, may become wise.

Sally Garratt

Introduction

'If only I had half a crown every time someone's said that to me,' my mother often says, 'I'd be a very rich woman'. I know exactly what she means. Recently, whenever I say that I am an independent consultant, someone is bound to say 'I don't see any future for me where I am – I'm thinking of going out on my own'. More and more people see self-employed consultancy as an alternative to traditional 'paid' employment and wish to emulate the life-style of successful freelancers. In fact, many freelancers, in common with some co-operatives, set up their businesses because they are running *away* from something, not because they are taking a positive step to achieve a well-defined aim. Such operations usually fail – for every two set up, probably only one will be successful. What, then, is the reality?

The reality is that most of these people find it difficult to reconcile the apparent freedom of the freelance consultant's lifestyle with the need for rigorous self-discipline. It means taking personal responsibility for *all* the support functions which were provided by previous employers. You have to become everyone, from the MD to the receptionist and storekeeper. You are totally responsible for everything – and that takes a lot of learning.

It is a great life when things are going well, and if you are of a temperament that thrives on uncertainty and can cope with long bursts of frenzied activity, periods away from home, occasional verbal abuse from clients, an erratic cash flow, the grind of unavoidable daily routine, and the feeling of elation experienced when working well with people who are pleased with what you are doing. Most people cannot do this, even when they earnestly wish to do so. Instead, they learn painfully just how dependent they are on an organization to structure their lives. I therefore dedicate this book to those who are determined to be independent, client-friendly, market-aware and self-developing.

There is no single clearly defined way to begin your new life as an independent consultant. Many people slowly build up a client base while still working for their employer, having perhaps negotiated a part-time position for a while. This is a good way of learning to cope with uncertainty and also gives you a fall-back position. Others may work with a client who suggests to them that it might be worthwhile becoming self-employed. The client might even offer the first project. I was fortunate that a friend, who was running a large project that he could not handle on his own, heard that I wanted to become independent and asked me to help him. 'But you don't even know whether I can do the work,' I protested. 'I know,' he replied, 'but I'm so desperate, I'll have to take a chance!' In my quieter moments, I still go hot and cold thinking about how things might not have turned out so well!

There are, however, a number of caveats to consider before taking the step towards independence. In the following pages I ask questions designed to make would-be consultants think hard about their motives, to be realistic about what being independent really means to them and their families, look at the infrastructure needed to make a consultancy operate smoothly and, above all, to look optimistically at all the positive aspects of being a free agent while, at the same time, still keeping an eye on possible pitfalls. Being self-employed is very much a matter of juggling the different aspects of your life to create the proper balance. On the one hand, you must build up the levels of expertise, experience and acknowledged competence which both enable you to give your clients a high-quality service and allow you to sustain a way of living to which you are, or wish to become, accustomed. On the other hand, you must also find time for the other priorities and responsibilities of your chosen way of life – family, home, friends, interests, leisure pursuits, or whatever.

This book is not about building a consultancy *business*. That requires a very different approach, in which the employment of others, the problems of overhead costs, capitalization, corporate taxations, earnings per share, dividends, and so on, easily take centre stage. That is not to say that self-employed consultants cannot grow equity in their work. Indeed, they have to operate as a one- or two-person mini-business, but that is not central to the acquisition of the life-style for which they have opted. That life-style does not suit everyone. However, for those intent on following such a path, this book will help you to establish a sound foundation on which to build your consultancy *practice*.

Who is this book aimed at?

I have written this book with a specific group of people in mind, but it is probably easier to say first who it is *not* for. It is not for people working in large consultancies where most of the issues of overheads, infrastructure, support services and who pays the bills are dealt with elsewhere. Neither is it for those young and inexperienced people who are bored with their first job or who think that being self-employed is the fastest route to fame and riches.

It is aimed at people, often professionals, who wish to, or have recently, set up as independent, self-employed practitioners. They have skills and knowledge to pass on to others and feel that they could do this more effectively outside a traditional company set-up. They probably have a proven track record within a commercial or industrial organization or an academic institution. They are people who are prepared to take the risks involved in setting up as an independent as well as having to cope with all aspects of running a small business. Working on your own or with only one or two other people means that you have to be the general manager of your business as well as a specialist in your chosen field.

The people I am thinking of will include *inter alia* those involved in the following areas: management consultancy and all aspects of human resource development; graphic and other design; film and video making; communications; financial, legal or medical services; engineering; security; beauty consultancy; construction services; advertising and public relations; and social services and other aspects of the public sector. Most of these people have specific skills and knowledge, gained over many years. They may have academic and professional qualifications. But, above all, if they are to be successful, they will have considerable practical experience. I do not expect that a recent graduate, aged twenty-one or thereabouts, will be in a position to become a successful independent consultant. Experience of working with other people, picking up tips on how to run a business and, most important, how to give advice effectively and efficiently – all this provides invaluable background to becoming a consultant.

Are you experienced enough to become a consultant?

In June 1989, Sue Thame was moved to write to the Newsletter of the Association for Management Education and Development about her concern that young people representing the profession of management consultants and developers are being pushed into work that is beyond their skills and experience. She wrote:

> Not so long ago, a top international management consultancy placed an advertisement in a UK newspaper to recruit 'education consultants'. It read 'We are looking for graduates with 3 to 5 years' experience and an impressive career record. People who have substantial knowledge and experience of instruction design, education, psychology and adult learning techniques'. The job would require incumbents to 'interview client management and identify the organisation's unique training needs' and 'design and develop appropriate training and teach client personnel to deliver the training'. They would 'be involved in all stages of business management from strategic planning to detailed implementation of changes'.
>
> Simple arithmetic puts the age of potential applicants at 25–28. What prodigies! To be able to take responsibility as consultants over such a wide range of issues at such an age! Is the advertisement an instance of 'never mind the quality, feel the width'?

Finally, as well as providing a framework for those wishing to become independent consultants, I have also included sections on basic management skills such as written communications and personal effectiveness. This is because many organizations do not give this essential grounding to their managers and because many schools fail to equip their students with the necessary reading, writing, listening and questioning skills for the workplace. They are part of the raft of competences you will need to develop as a consultant.

I am writing this book from the point of view of a management consultant (although I have also worked in design practices, training departments of large organizations and as a teacher of adults). Most of the examples are, therefore, from the world I know best. My contacts in other fields assure me that the basic principles hold true and may be applied to most types of consultancy. No matter what your specialist area is, I hope that this book will help you to become successful and stay successful – whatever that word means to you.

1 Why be a Consultant?

Many people who express the wish to become self-employed have ambivalent views about making this important move. On the one hand, they say 'I'll be able to do what I want, when I want and how I want – it'll be great', but then, on the other hand, they think 'It's such a risk – suppose it doesn't work out?'. Both feelings are natural, and it is possible to be realistic about what you may or may not do while minimizing the risks through careful planning and preparation.

What is a consultant?

It may be useful to spend a few minutes considering what being a consultant means and identifying different types of consulting.

The Institute of Management Consultants defines a management consultant as follows:

> A Management Consultant is an independent and qualified person who provides a professional service to business, public and other undertakings by:
>
> (a) identifying and investigating problems concerned with strategy, policy, markets, organization, procedures and methods;
> (b) formulating recommendations for appropriate action by factual investigation and analysis with due regard for broader management and business implications;
> (c) discussing and agreeing with the client the most appropriate course of action;

(d) providing assistance where required by the client to implement his recommendations.

For the purposes of this book a 'consultant' is someone other people ask for advice, and look to for guidance, instruction or information – someone external to the work group or organization with whom to co-operate on and discuss a wide range of issues relating to the business. This gives an aspect to the nature of consultancy which may be quite different from the view of those who see it simply as going into an organization, telling the board what is wrong and how to put it right, and who then, claiming a huge fee, go away leaving behind an eternally grateful client.

Why do people employ consultants?

Consultants are used by organizations and individuals for several reasons. At first sight, it may seem strange for companies to employ outsiders to tackle a task which could be done by internal people, and to pay them well to do it, but consider the following reasons:

● Some organizations may not have the necessary expertise amongst their existing staff to solve a specific problem.
● The expertise may be there but the appropriate people may not be able to fit the assignment into their timetables.
● Even if the right people could take on the task, they themselves might recognize that sometimes an outsider can see problems in a new light and bring a fresh perspective to them.
● Company politics may be such that a disinterested outsider's opinion might be more acceptable than that of a staff member.
● A third party, such as an organization's bank, may insist on an impartial view of a particular issue.
● An outsider can always be blamed if things go wrong, and thus keep intact the social bonds which exist in the organization.

Approaches to consulting

In an article 'From Expertise to Contingency: Changes in the Nature of Consulting' (1981), Bob Garratt identifies three styles in consulting practice: expertise consulting; process consulting; and contingent consulting. Each of these three types of approach is distinct and, if appropriate for the circumstances, equally valid. It is important to know in which area you are operating as the skills needed for each are different, and you need to understand the expectations of the client and the employees you are working with.

Expertise consulting

One use of the 'expertise consulting' approach is when an acknowledged *expert* in a specific area is asked into an organization to provide a solution to an already identified problem; for example, the need to design and install a word processing system or a new accounting system. In such a case, the consultant's main contact is with the person who asked him in to look at the problem – the client. Although the people directly concerned with the introduction of the new system (the problem-owners) may be interviewed, the strongest link is with the client.

This approach may also take the form of a training course where the expert will pass on knowledge or skills to a group of people, either in-company or on a public programme. Once the course is completed, the consultant will not usually have any further contact with the participants. All a consultant can therefore hope for in this 'sheep dip' approach is that some of what has been thrown at the participants will be remembered and put to use after the programme. A good trainer can pass on valuable knowledge and skills, but it is debatable whether this ability alone is sufficient to make a success of consulting if there is to be an element of two-way communication as implied in the definitions.

In his later work, Bob Garratt has likened this approach to surgery; that is, an operation that gives an immediate result but which cannot always be guaranteed to provide a permanent solution to the problem. It is a drastic, often irreversible step but, used in conjunction with other consulting styles, it can serve a useful purpose.

Process consulting

Next, a method which provides a balance to the logical, rational and often arms-length style of expertise consulting. It involves people much more in their social processes, that is, the feelings and behaviours concerned with a range of managerial problem-solving processes. They often experience a release of energy previously unknown to them. Working with the emotions in this way may also go beyond the brief envisaged by the original client and leave the participants fired up with ideas, and with confidence and enthusiasm that the organization cannot control or accommodate back at the workplace. The relationship between consultant and the problem-owners becomes quite close during the time they are working together. This can sometimes work against the interests of the organization as a whole if the participants become alienated from the client.

Rather than surgery, this style of consulting may be compared with therapy. As such, it usually needs a complementary approach to enable participants to develop their newly discovered potential in coping with the 'real' world of their organization and the problems they face.

Contingent consulting

The aim of the contingent consultant is to make himself redundant as quickly as possible! This contradicts the conviction held by some clients (and consultants) that consultants are in business to maximize their fees. The contingent consultant endeavours to make optimal use of the resources already held in an organization in the form of its employees and their experience. As Bob Garratt writes: 'It attempts to integrate the expertise and process practices when appropriate to the progression of the organisation's problem . . . relying on the asking of high-quality questions and developing an information-based approach to problem-solving.'

The consultant, whether internal or external, is neither surgeon nor therapist and is used rarely, rather like small doses of homeopathic medicine given only when needed. The strongest relationship here is that between the formal client and the problem-owner, and the resulting team is therefore highly effective in working together in identifying and solving problems.

Many consultants find this 'contingency' approach disquieting. Facing a situation where answering unpredictable questions and demands is the norm places too great a stress on those consultants who cannot call on the necessary range of skills or breadth of experience. In the area of management development, while the consultant is looked upon by the participants as a resource, he limits the amount of formal input and regards the ability to design the appropriate learning processes as one of the important contributions he can make to the organization and its employees.

It may seem strange that, in using a consultant to help solve a problem, the client is not buying that consultant's expert knowledge of the subject to unravel the problem, but rather his intelligence and naivety. In many situations, the issues that look like technical puzzles (yet which cannot be solved by technical staff) are symptoms of a managerial problem. In this case, therefore, finding the solution often depends on the ability to reframe the question in such a way that the client's values are made explicit.

To explain this a little further – if you are faced with a puzzle, the solution is already implicit in the statement describing it. It may be complex but it is there. In describing the problem, on the other hand, you state the parameters within which it could be solved, which include the values of the client. This often requires the 'reframing' ability – the professional skill to rise above the problem and view it in various different ways.

The contingency approach also presents problems to those clients who expect from their consultants the traditional response of 'I'll tell you what to do, and you can go away and do it'.

Finally, whichever approach is used – expertise, process or contingency consulting – the test of its quality is whether the client feels at the end of the exercise that the relationship has been one of colleagues acting in a participative way to resolve organizational issues.

Exploding the myths of independent consultancy

There are several popular myths about the advantages of being an independent consultant. They need to be dispelled at once.

'It's money for old rope'

If you want to last longer than a couple of years, this approach is fatal. Most consultants I know have never worked harder in their lives, particularly during the early years.

Clients are generally demanding, and rightly so, for they are buying your expertise at high rates. While clever marketing may get you single assignments, your true worth is shown by referrals and repeat work. You may complete a project, but if it is not of good quality, delivered on time and to cost, you will never work for that client again and she will certainly never endorse or recommend your work to anyone else.

The popular misconception that you can earn a lot of money doing very little may have been perpetuated by jealous employed people, but there is, of course, another side to the story. Each new client and each new assignment means you have to prove yourself – very few clients are willing to hire you solely on your past reputation. Nevertheless, this does provide a fine opportunity for the consultant to grow and learn from each project. Here is the ideal chance to assess and adapt your techniques on a continuing basis, to build on existing skills and knowledge, and, over the years, to develop an individual, flexible and sought-after approach to consulting.

'I'll earn much more as a consultant than as an executive'

Clients believe this myth, too! A consultant's daily rates may seem high, but if you break down a senior manager's salary into daily rates, and include all the benefits and overheads, there is not much to choose between them. An important thing to remember is that consultants do not earn if they are not working. The same cannot be said of many managers in organizations!

In the long term, other benefits of being independent will probably be more important than what you earn.

'My time's my own' or 'I'll be able to work when I want to'

That is the theory, but at the beginning most consultants cannot be too particular about when they work. You must be clear in your mind which types of project you will not undertake and which categories of client you will not work for. However, you will probably have to show some flexibility about *when* you work, at least until you are well established.

Planning your time is an important aspect of a consultant's life. Even if you have learnt some techniques in your previous job, these will need to be adapted for life as an independent operator. Not only will you have to plan current and potential work, but you will also need to leave space for winning new work. Unless you are very lucky, this will not just appear.

It is typical for new consultants to say 'Yes' to everything and then to realize at the end of a few months that they are exhausted, have not kept their filing or techniques up to date and do not seem to have followed their good intentions about having holidays or weekends, playing golf, spending time with the family or reading the newspapers and magazines. When a consultant becomes known and respected, clients are more flexible and usually a compromise can be reached. 'I really can't manage that week but the next one's free – could we start then?'. The panic that makes you refuse nothing subsides after a while as your confidence grows in your ability to pace yourself, schedule work and minimize the number of surprises in your life. At the beginning, however, you will have to work long and hard to establish yourself in the eyes of others, to build your own confidence and knowledge, and to set up workable systems and routines. Eventually, the short-term sacrifices should result in a strong foundation on which you can build longer-term success and its benefits.

As you become more established you can more easily design your life-style. For example, I like to ensure that I spend time in London, China/Hong Kong and France each year. My clients seem to respect this and acknowledge that they receive better advice because of the breadth of my experiences.

'*I won't be answerable to anyone else*'

If this is your reason for becoming a consultant, you will be very short of assignments. The client provides a brief, you perform a service and you are duly paid. The quality of clients varies enormously. The good ones will know what they want, may negotiate on some points such as timing, will perhaps remain open to suggestion on parts of the brief and will be prepared to discuss aspects of the assignment without casting doubt on your abilities. The not-so-good clients will expect you to know everything, will not brief you adequately (perhaps hiding ignorance on their part), will argue every point and query every expense on the invoice, and will generally give you the impression that you are there only because they do not have the time to do the job personally. In spite of all this, you have to answer to the client for your work.

Many of the pitfalls may be avoided by careful discussion and preparation at the outset – the 'contracting' process. There are always the awkward customers – clients who do not seem to know what they want and often change their minds, clients who quietly add bits to the original brief, clients who seem to resent your presence. Mostly, you will have to grin and bear it, and, after a while, you will develop a feeling for the people with whom you will enjoy working. You do not have to like the people who hire you – although it helps – but you will soon recognize the characteristics of those who will bring you only grief.

'I'm looking forward to all those expenses-paid trips'

Usually the glamour of travelling at someone else's expense is a great attraction for the would-be consultant. Some of it is exciting, giving you the opportunity to visit places you have not seen before, but do not pin your hopes on exotic foreign locations, it is just as likely to be Southampton as Singapore. In any case, you probably will not see much more than your hotel room, the inside of a taxi, your client's office and all sorts of indifferent restaurants.

There is a positive side to travelling, of course, and over the past thirteen years, my husband and I have built up a client base in the Far East which means we travel there frequently and regularly. We try to plan our work assignments there in such a way that we have some free time to visit places we would not normally see, using Hong Kong as our base.

Travelling long distances can be stressful and some people find it easier to cope with than others. Later in the book there are some suggestions on managing these assignments, for those who may find it useful. Wherever you go, it is a chance to meet new people, see different countryside, townscapes and architecture, observe different customs and standards of living, and perhaps gain a new perspective on the way you tackle your project. It all helps your 'reframing' skills.

'I'll be able to tell everyone what to do'

The changing nature of consultancy means that clients are becoming less open to being told what is best for them. They are increasingly likely to ask pertinent questions, and the more discerning ones want you to help them identify a problem and find a solution which they feel they can own rather than have you produce a glib, ready-made answer.

In some areas of consultancy, it is possible to decide what type of consultant you will be. For example, consultants involved in management training and development may operate in one of three ways (or a combination of the three): expertise, process or contingency (as described on pages 2–5). Certainly, the high-handed attitude typified by the 'Don't argue with me, I know about these things' approach is rarely tolerated today. Some consultants, for instance in the design world, may feel that their own standards are being compromised when a client will not accept what to the trained eye is an aesthetically pleasing and visually balanced piece of work. The essence of good consultancy is building up a relationship of trust with the client so that disagreements and misunderstandings may be brought out into the open, discussed and resolved. There is no advantage to be gained in refusing to give way on any point.

'I can claim everything back on tax'

If only that were so. It is quite clear what may be or may not be claimed on tax and this is where a taxation adviser will be of enormous help. Large expense-account lunches are not only bad for your health, but will also cost you a lot of money and are *not* reclaimable. (See Chapter 5.)

'I've been promised plenty of work, so that will be no problem'

Many people promise work to the budding consultant, but often as a sign of support and encouragement rather than as a firm contract. If the work exists, it may be only a small job and there will not necessarily be more to follow. Unless you have a substantial amount of money to support you for a year or so, before you start as an independent consultant you need to be sure that an adequate income is guaranteed from definite projects to cover at least part of your costs. This could be done by some part-time teaching or working as a sub-contractor to another consultant. Do not be lured by vague promises or assume that a casual passing remark means a firm commitment. Work is sometimes cancelled and postponed, often through no fault of the client, and even if you receive a cancellation fee, it may not compensate fully for wasted preparation time or for the inability to replace that particular project with another job immediately in order to keep your cash flow balanced.

'I'm feeling pretty relaxed about it – something's bound to turn up'

Such a casual approach to consultancy will probably result in failure. Plans have to be made, projects scheduled, strategies and visions formulated and markets explored, if you are to be successful. As your reputation grows, unsolicited work may come in, but you can never rely on it. Most consultants would agree that, even if the first steps have been well thought through, it may still take four or five years to become thoroughly established. If you do not do your homework and are not prepared to work hard, you have little chance of making a go of consultancy.

'It's the best thing to do, now I've been made redundant'

It is difficult to transfer immediately from being an employee to being a consultant. The skills of consulting are usually different from those used as an employee and need to be developed consciously over time.

As someone who has been made redundant, what you normally have to offer is expertise from a limited number of previous jobs. Technical expertise is something that employees in other organizations are likely to possess, and it is expertise that people from other organizations will probably reject. What they want is someone who will listen first, reflect on a wide range of previous experience and future options second, ask good, discerning questions of the experts third, and then counsel and probe until the clients devise a solution to which they will commit themselves. As this is not a usual process for the managers, it takes some considerable skill to master even stage one, that is, to stop talking and listen. God gave us two eyes, two ears and one mouth and they should be used in that proportion!

According to a recent survey, 'the chances of success appear to be better for people who choose to enter consultancy after thoughtful preparation than for those pitched into it by the sack'. (GMS Consultancy, 1990).

What are your motives?

Your motives for wanting to be an independent consultant must be clear. It is not wrong to aspire to a certain life-style but, as a consultant, it will not come without hard work. Indeed, if you choose to work in, for example, the voluntary sector, you will not be able to charge high rates, so living in the lap of luxury is obviously not your highest priority. Contrary to popular belief, to be a consultant is not synonymous with being rich, so you must decide early on what it is you're looking for. Is it any of the following?

- *Fulfilment* To be completely involved in your work and satisfied that you have done a good job.
- *Independence* To have a choice of what you do; being your own boss.
- *Variety* Of work and clients.
- *Meeting people* Of all types from many different types of organization.
- *Wealth* If you make the conscious choice of targeting only money-making projects.
- *Glamour* Becoming well known and in demand as a 'personality'.
- *Status* Having your opinion respected and in demand, as well as showing the material signs of success.
- *Revenge* Getting your own back for all the times you have had to do what you were told or were criticized unjustly.
- *Power* Being able to influence powerful clients.

You should look honestly into your reasons for wanting to become an independent consultant and then you can be realistic about the hard work involved in setting up and maintaining your practice.

Using the list above as a starting point, write down on the next page your own motives for wanting to become a consultant.

What are my motives for wanting to become a consultant?

The reasons people give for becoming consultants are many and varied. For example, the following four statements show the range:

- 'I don't like working for other people. I don't like the structure, the authority. I like to make my own choices.'
- 'I was made redundant from my full-time job.'
- 'When I wanted to change jobs, companies wanted applicants with a straight, well-defined career line. Mine was too wiggly!'
- 'The nature of my personality and the way I view organizations means I operate more effectively when I can be *in* them but not *of* them.'

When we become consultants, we have ideas about what the advantages will be. When I asked some well-established freelances what they liked most about being a consultant, the common themes were 'freedom', 'variety' and 'self-reliance'. The following five statements were typical:

- 'I like not having anyone else to blame if things go wrong.'
- 'Being able to say "No, I don't want to do that," and not having to refer to anyone else.'
- 'I can develop myself in ways I want.'
- 'Managing myself, my own situation, my own time – falling back on myself.'
- 'My afternoon snooze!'

It may be difficult to envisage what the downside of being independent will be, except perhaps the uncertainty about your financial situation. When I asked several consultants what they liked least about being on their own, their responses followed a similar pattern. They are summed up as follows:

- 'Uncertainty of the future.'
- 'Not getting regular cheques or being paid on time.'
- 'Being away from home.'
- 'Sometimes the loneliness and isolation – not having someone to bounce ideas off.'

2 The Nature of Consultancy

Consultants should be aware of their own strengths and weaknesses and how relevant they are to this type of work if they are to be effective in the role. You should take a long, hard look at what you have to offer in terms of skills, knowledge, talents and personal qualities, and measure them.

You can do this by completing the questionnaires or inventories which are administered by licensed trainers and which show how you behave in certain situations; for example, when things are going well or when you are under pressure. There are also career analysts who will spend time with you and give you an assessment of the areas in which your particular skills might be employed. There are books on the market which will offer you many kinds of help and advice if you wish to set up your own consultancy.

You can also build a framework for yourself which will allow you to assess: the areas in which you have much to offer; the experience which you may need to expand; and the skills you should acquire. It is important to keep a balance between exaggerating the depth of your experience, and not giving it enough prominence. Skills and qualities come from a broad range of activities, not just from your working life. For example, voluntary work often produces expertise which is extremely useful elsewhere. When I acted as secretary to the management committee of an adventure playground, I learned a great deal about negotiating with the local council at a time of extensive cuts in grants and resources. I was also able to develop the

15

skills associated with meetings and committees, as well as having to recruit playworkers, monitor their training, carry out disciplinary procedures, and try to motivate local residents to join the committee. All of this was different from my other work experience and has added a new dimension to some of my consultancy projects.

It is useful to look at all the activities that make up the total sum of your life and extract what you have learned from each of these. In this way, you will be able to assess where your particular strengths lie and what you need to do to consolidate these positive points. This analysis will also help you to recognize the areas in which you do not perform so well, and you can then decide whether it is worth spending time and effort to improve them, or not to offer them at all as part of your service.

I thought about the skills and qualities needed to become a successful independent consultant and then wondered if they would be viewed differently by consultants and their clients. In early 1990, I asked some clients what they looked for in the consultants they employed and I asked consultants what they thought the clients were looking for. From their answers to this small survey I compiled the following lists:

Skills

From 65 statements from clients and 18 from consultants, the priorities given to skills were as follows (the numbers in brackets show how many respondents mentioned each skill):

	Clients' answers	*Consultants' answers*
1	Self-organization and discipline (10)	Listening (5)
2	Interpersonal and motivation (9)	Customer service (5)
3	Analytic/diagnostic/clear thinker (7)	Analytic/diagnostic/clear thinker (4)
4	Verbal and written (6)	Verbal and written (1)
5	Customer service (6)*	Interpersonal and motivation (1)
6	Experienced/up-to-date (6)	Questioning (1)
7	Creative/innovative (5)	Self-organization and discipline (1)

8   Expert (5)
9   Listening (4)
10 Questioning (4)
11 Organization politics (2)
12 Answering (1)

* 'Customer care' includes such statements as: added value; nurturing; updating; keeping in touch; carrying through; finishing off; being flexible and responsive.

Qualities

From 40 statements from clients and 12 from consultants, the priorities given to qualities were as follows (the numbers in brackets show how many respondents mentioned each quality:

Clients' answers	*Consultants' answers*
1 Empathy/awareness (12)	Integrity/honesty (4)
2 Integrity/honesty (6)	Thorough interest in what client is talking about (1)
3 Flexibility (5)	Flexibility (1)
4 Open and sharing (4)	Patient (1)
5 Well-mannered/acceptable (3)	Well/mannered (1)
6 Friendly but firm/ confident (2)	Provocative (1)
7 Intelligent (2)	Not embarrassed to talk about fees (1)
8 Reliable (2)	Good-natured (1)
9 Imaginative (1)	Imaginative (1)
10 Able to accept criticism (1)	
11 Constructive (1)	
12 Pragmatic (1)	

Warning

It is important to remember that, if a strength is taken to extremes, it may be perceived as a weakness by others. For example, great attention to detail, seen by you as proof of your analytical and careful nature, may be perceived as nitpicking by a client; the self-confidence, of which you are so proud, may come across as arrogance to other people. Different clients will see your strengths in different lights. Use behaviour appropriate to the occasion.

In the same way, different words may have several meanings depending upon your viewpoint. For instance, a consultant may use the word 'flexible' to mean 'willing to discuss various approaches to a problem', whereas a client might see it as 'able to come round to my point of view without too much argument'.

The following checklists incorporate the skills and qualities from the above lists. Match yourself against these by grading yourself on a scale, one to ten with one low and ten high, against each skill or quality. You could also ask someone else close to you – partner, friend or colleague – to repeat the same exercise, scoring you against each word. This may be painful, but it is very useful to find out how others perceive you.

Skills

	Self	A.N. Other
1 Self-organization and discipline:		

- time management
- systems and routines
- meetings

2 Interpersonal

- social
- motivation
- energy/enthusiasm

3 Communication

- verbal
- voice
- listening
- questioning
- presentation
- appearance
- body language

4   Professional/technical

- appropriate qualifications
- training
- depth of knowledge
- breadth of experience

Now complete the chart on qualities, also grading yourself on a scale
one to ten and ask someone else to do it, too.

Qualities

		Self	A.N. Other
1	Empathy/awareness		
2	Integrity/honesty		
3	Logical/clear thinking		
4	Flexibility		
5	Open and sharing		
6	Well-mannered/acceptable		
7	Unflappable		
8	Patient		
9	Confident		
10	Intelligent		
11	Reliable		
12	Good-natured		
13	Practical		
14	Imaginative		
15	Resilient		
16	Pragmatic		
17	Others:		

Clients' views of consultants

Most clients have strong views about the type of people they prefer to use as consultants and many have learned from past experiences, both good and bad. As a consultant, you will benefit from understanding what your clients' attitudes are and, during any negotiations, it will be worth finding out about their previous experiences with consultants, if any.

Some of the general comments made by clients about consultants in my survey were as follows:

- 'I am deeply suspicious of consultants with a defined product. It feels like a solution in search of a problem.'
- 'I am wary of people who call themselves consultants and set up a one-man business following redundancy'.
- 'I look for consultants who are well established, have a strong client base, are successful and are consultants through active choice.'
- 'I have failed twice when employing consultants and both times it was for the same reasons. First, the consultant came with a course that he was not prepared to tailor for our organization. Secondly, the courses and the consultants were totally inflexible; they had a timetable and stuck to it rigidly. The very worst aspect of both of these consultants was that they lacked a sense of humour and couldn't cope with fairly lively groups. They became defensive and then autocratic, which in turn caused the groups to turn against them and they lost credibility.'
- 'The "fit" of the consultant's style with the client is crucial to the effectiveness of the role.'

3 Organization and Location

Running their own company is the ambition of many people who see success in terms of being the boss, but there are many ways of setting up a business. The nature of the business may determine the form of your organization. You should be aware of the pros and cons of working as a sole trader, in a partnership or as a limited company. This chapter examines these three structures and also looks at the options open to you regarding the location of your office.

Legal structure

The three types of legal structure usually considered by consultants setting up on their own are: sole trader; partnership; and limited company. Your situation will determine which structure is the most advantageous for you and you should therefore speak to your legal and financial advisers who will help you decide which is best.

Sole trader

Consultants often start off as sole traders as this requires the minimum of formalities. There are no legal agreements or complex documentation to complete and costs are therefore kept down. A government licence is required for those operating employment agencies or providing financial services.

As no one else is involved, the decision-making process is simple (but not necessarily easy). This again emphasizes the need for a consultant to have sound experience upon which reliable decisions may be made, as there is no one else to discuss matters with. The sole trader does not have to ask anyone about how capital or profits will be spent or invested.

In its favour, accounting is relatively simple and, as the overheads are low, you can have greater flexibility in pricing your fees and covering your costs. There are, of course, some disadvantages to becoming a sole trader, and the consultant's temperament and readiness to take risks will determine his willingness to operate in this way. The main disadvantage is that, in law, the owner and the business are deemed to be one and the same, and unlimited liability means that the individual's personal assets may be seized in case of outstanding debts or liabilities.

Partnership

'A partnership is more difficult to get out of than a marriage and more costly' is a familiar quote!

A partnership is the association of two or more people in business, sharing risks and profits and 'being jointly and severally liable'. The agreement between the individuals may be verbal or written. Partnership deeds need to be carefully drafted – it is strongly advised that you have a written agreement – and good legal advice needs to be taken, as any one person leaving a partnership will destroy the whole. It is, therefore, as important to stipulate how things are dissolved as how they are formed.

There are obvious advantages in pooling not only skills, knowledge and other resources, but also capital. A partnership should offer a wider range of expertise than a sole trader, and partners must therefore be able to offer complementary skills to clients. Some consultants need to know that there are other people around with whom they can discuss various issues, such as the approach to an assignment or to brainstorm different ideas. For such people, the isolation of being a sole trader is not an attractive proposition.

Unlimited liability applies to all partners who are individually and collectively liable for all the partnership's debts and liabilities. A partnership, therefore, carries more serious implications, commercially and personally, than sole trader status since the unwise actions of one partner can affect the livelihood of the others and their families. Also, if a partnership breaks up, some issues can become very messy, especially that of 'goodwill'. There are horror stories of widows being pursued by the tax inspector over notional goodwill – and being bankrupted in the process!

Working with other people, even if you are convinced that you will get on well under any circumstances, is another area of potential discord. If you are determined to go ahead with a partnership, it is important to have an agreement drawn up which specifies the role and contribution of each partner in all aspects of the business. Should the partnership break down, for whatever reason, there will be difficulties, involving legal and administrative expenses, and the situation may lead to serious personal anguish. Without a formal agreement, the breakdown may become drawn out and acrimonious. For this reason, it is crucial to make sure that each partner's duties and responsibilities, contribution to and drawings from the business, are clearly defined.

One way of finding out if this is the route you want to take is to work together on one or two projects on a one-off basis, with a written contract about roles and responsibilities, timings, payments, and so on, drawn up before you enter a formal partnership. In this way you will find out what it is like working together, as this trial period will help highlight areas of difficulty, personality problems or different ways of operating.

Limited company

The third option, setting up a limited company, with or without share capital, is probably not so attractive to an independent operator at the outset. There are more government regulations covering this option. Companies are therefore more expensive to establish and operate because of the large amount of documentation which has to be dealt with, and they usually carry higher overhead costs. They also have to comply with the Companies Act 1989, which includes requirements for audited accounts.

Shareholders' liability is limited, but there are exceptions and directors are now personally liable for their actions, especially in the case of fraud. These aspects are dealt with in the Insolvency Act 1986. However, on the positive side there are tax advantages available for a limited company which do not apply to sole traders or partnerships. (See Chapter 5).

Whatever you think would be best for you, do not make a move without exploring all the alternatives with your legal and financial advisers. It is difficult to keep up to date with all the changes in taxation, insurance policies and other legislation, so leave that to the experts and give yourself time to do what you want to do.

Where will you work from?

The obvious place for many independent consultants to set up their offices is their home. For some, the aim is to move into a separate office when the business is established; for others, the intention is to stay small and keep overheads to a minimum.

Working from home

Working from home is an attractive proposition for several reasons, although there are, of course, some disadvantages.

Travelling

You do away with the daily grind of commuting. Travelling to see clients can often be arranged to miss rush hours. Even being squashed up against other commuters doesn't seem quite so bad if you know it is only going to happen once in a while. Remember though, that consultants often have to spend several days away from home at a time. For those with families and close personal ties this can present some difficulties and is a subject that should be discussed in depth before you set up on your own.

Costs

It is possible to keep costs to a minimum if you work from home. You save on rent and travelling and the use of part of your home may be set against tax. In many countries, however, local taxes or rates may be chargeable, so find out informally the approach your local authority takes to the use of your home as your office.

Nearness to work and family

For the most part, being near to both work and family is fine. Just going into another room in the house to work removes all the stress of travelling. Being around when the children come home and generally having more access to them, feeling comfortable with your surroundings, and not having to dress up for work if you do not want to – are all common reasons for not working in a separate location.

At the same time, the distractions when working from home are many and varied. The opportunities for displacement activities abound. It takes a great deal of self-discipline to admit to yourself the difference between a legitimate need to have a break and putting off doing a difficult and boring business task by persuading yourself that washing the car is more important.

For those with families, it is good to be more involved and accessible, but young children can distract you and be distracted by you. Again, this is something that should be discussed with your partner, so that the reality of having you working at home is faced.

It is tempting to spend more time at your desk if you do not have to go out to work, and easy access to the office means that workaholics often work even longer hours than they did when employed. Most people would agree, however, that more time spent working does not necessarily mean a proportionate quality of output. For the sake of your health and self-development you must achieve the correct balance between time spent working and time at home or at leisure. (See Chapter 13.)

Meeting clients

It is usual to go to a client's office for meetings but occasionally this may not be convenient. If the consultant's home is easily accessible, most clients do not seem to mind going there, but there are obvious problems if home is many miles away. In such a case, it is useful to have access to a meeting place in the centre of the city or in the nearest town. Hotels in business centres usually have rooms to hire or, if the subject is not too confidential, hotel lounges or coffee bars can be pleasant places to sit and talk. If you are a member of a club or a professional body, you may be able to hire a room for the required period from them.

An office away from home

When first setting up, it is not always economically feasible to rent, lease or buy office space. There are, however, various alternatives available for those who cannot or do not wish to work from home. The most serious commitment would be to buy premises, and the feasibility of this will depend on issues such as cost, availability, suitability, and real need. Most consultants do not invest in property in this way when they are starting up, although some insist it is necessary to help create an asset which they can cash in for their pension. Leasing office space requires sound advice from your accountant and a solicitor used to dealing with commercial leases. Be sure that you avoid restrictions which will hinder your work or not allow you to sublet if you so wish. You should remember that there will be no additional services available so all this will be extra expenditure. Renting space is the option most usually adopted by consultants, and one of the most flexible arrangements to consider is the managed workspace.

Managed workspace or working community

A popular way to rent space is to base your business in a managed workspace. The most flexible type is where you pay a rate per square foot per annum and you may increase or decrease your space according to your needs. As an example, one working community in Chiswick, West London, charges £35 or £37 per square foot per annum and this includes rent and rates, service charge, heating, lighting, cleaning, carpeting, central switchboard and reception, conference rooms, tea and coffee and a franking postal service. (There are also workshops available at £23 or £24 per square foot per annum).

Another long-established managed workspace in Covent Garden, central London, charges £70 per week for approximately 80 square feet. This covers the space and telephone, plus tea and coffee, use of conference rooms and reception. Also available in the building are secretarial services, printing, designers and bookkeepers, all of which are available to provide any necessary services at market rates. Licensees pay rent quarterly in advance and in addition are charged for telephone and fax.

A more recent establishment in Islington, North London, charges £29.50 per square foot per annum. The rent is £15 per square foot and there is no premium. The uniform business charge and all services are charged at cost, currently £14.50 per square foot per annum. The services include central heating, power and light, daily office cleaning, use of meeting rooms, kitchens (including tea and coffee), building insurance and maintenance, full-time reception and message taking, mail collection, security and on-site management. There is also an in-house subsidized restaurant. A licence normally runs for a one-year period and three months' notice is required to terminate the agreement during the licence period.

Gina Goodwin of Tavistock Consultants has recently published *The Tavistock Handbook and Directory of UK Business Centres and Managed Workspaces* (£9.95). She can be contacted at 45 Tavistock Terrace, London N19 4BZ, tel: 071 272 4278.

What determines the location?

Different types of work and different structures may determine the location of a business. For example, graphic designers, management consultants or freelance writers could easily work from home, away from a town or city centre, especially if they have the necessary technology installed in their offices. As long as they are prepared to travel to convenient meeting places from time to time and have access to support and back-up, being isolated should not have a detrimental affect on their business. An independent film maker, on the other hand, would find it hard to operate far away from access to facilities such as editing suites or recording studios. The growth of tele-commuting has meant that some consultants, such as software writers, have much more flexibility in choosing where they are based.

One school of thought says that potential clients will be deterred by consultants who work from home as they are obviously single operators. I have not found this to be the case and neither have any of the independent consultants I have spoken to or worked with. Clients generally now have broader experience of working with consultants and are aware of the different circumstances in which the large consultancies and the smaller independent practices operate. They do, however, have expectations of reasonable comfort and style; introducing them to an untidy room, with a child howling in the background, the dog running out of control in the garden and the telephone constantly ringing, is unlikely to promote your services. You will be remembered – but for all the wrong reasons!

4   Using Advisers

A consultant's advisers are so important to the smooth running of a business, however small, that it is vital to employ the right ones. This not only means those who are qualified and experienced enough to do a competent job for you but also those you like and feel comfortable working with. In this chapter the contribution of the following advisers will be discussed:

- bank manager
- accountant/taxation adviser
- legal
- insurance
- other consultants
- professional body
- designers
- personnel
- travel
- health

Bank manager

'Train your bank manager' was one of the first pieces of advice I was given as a consultant. It certainly is worth making an effort to spend time deciding where to base your account(s) and in getting to know your manager. While the bank nearest to you is the most convenient, it may not be the most suitable for your needs. For example, a small branch with little experience of self-employed people might not provide all the services you would expect, although a far-sighted manager in such a branch may well be very willing to accommodate you and add a little variety to his life. A very large branch in a busy city centre may not be prepared to devote what you consider to be the appropriate attention to your comparatively small interests unless it offers specialist advice and services to small businesses.

Therefore, weigh up the advantages and disadvantages of size, personal attention, specialist services and ease of access when choosing a bank. Talk to the bank manager before you place your account, even if you have banked there for years, and discuss the special needs of an independent consultant. Find out what sort of information the manager will need from you to keep him happy; for example, regular cash flow forecasts to reassure him that, although there may not be much money in your account at the moment, it will be coming in next month. Keep the bank manager informed of the different projects you are involved in. If you are going to be away for an unusually long time or if you are expecting a particularly large bill, let the manager know. Do not let him be faced with any unpleasant surprises, because bank managers like to know what is going on and will send you rude and costly letters if they do not.

The role of banks and bank managers has changed dramatically over the last few years. They now offer a wide range of services, many of which are now specifically designed for small business and the self-employed. So ask questions, and make sure that you know exactly what the bank can do for you. Handle the bank manager as you would a client – listen to what he needs from you, provide it with alacrity, and he, in turn, should look after you. Bank managers can also be a useful source of new clients, provided, of course, that they have a high regard for you and your practice.

Accountant/taxation adviser

Accountancy and tax advice are not necessarily the same thing. If you keep simple accounts, you may prefer to concentrate on taxation advice and seek an accountant who specialises in taxation. (See Chapter 5.)

Make sure, though, that you work with a properly qualified accountant who will be able to give you advice on future plans for your business, on tax-related affairs, and on preparing business plans. An accountant should be consulted about how to prepare and submit profit and loss accounts, balance sheets and cash flow forecasts. (See Chapter 5.) This information may also be available from your bank manager.

Bookkeeping services may be provided by an accountant or you may go to an independent bookkeeper. Some independent consultants keep their own books and submit them to their accountant/taxation adviser at the end of the financial year for their professional attention and completion. This takes some more of the famous self-discipline, as you really should do the accounts every day rather than wait to complete the books at the end of the year.

Legal advice

Whoever looks after your legal affairs must be a specialist in small businesses, who will understand the particular issues affecting consultants. You will not need to use a lawyer's services much in setting up as a sole trader but it would be wise to employ one if you are drawing up contracts or a partnership agreement. If you take the step of becoming a company, your legal adviser will obviously play a most important part in helping you avoid all the potential pitfalls of commercial law.

Should you become involved in writing contracts for your clients, or if any clients prepare their own, you will probably wish to have them drawn up or checked by someone who specializes in contract law. This may be the same person who looks after your other interests. If not, it may be another lawyer within the same practice or one who is recommended by your usual adviser.

Again, establishing a good relationship with your legal adviser(s) is important as, on the few (we hope) occasions when you will work together, speed and co-operation may be of the essence.

Intellectual property law is a growing area which will impinge on consultants' sphere of activity more and more. This whole subject is covered in more detail in Chapter 9.

Insurance

You could draw up your own insurance portfolio by reading all the journals in the library, but it would take a great deal of time. The safest approach is to go to an adviser and, in the UK, there are two types to choose from. There are 'appointed agents' or 'independent financial advisers' (IFAs) and no one person can have a dual role.

Appointed agents represent one insurance company and legally they can sell only the products of that company. If the company does not have the full range of products, the agent cannot sell you one that is unsuitable. These agents in the United Kingdom must be members of the Life Assurance Unit Trust Regulatory Organisation (LAUTRO).

Independent financial advisers (IFAs) can only recommend the product that is best for you. They must be impartial and must give 'best advice'. IFAs in the United Kingdom are usually members of The Financial Intermediaries, Managers and Brokers Regulatory Association (FIMBRA) and the big firms may become registered with the Securities Investment Board direct.

Other sources of advice are the banks and building societies, both of which may be tied to one insurance company. Solicitors and accountants are recognized professional bodies and do not have to be governed by FIMBRA or LAUTRO. Some large firms of account-ants have set up their own broking arm and others will be able to introduce you to an IFA.

In building up an insurance portfolio, there are two aspects to consider – protection and investment.

Protection

It is absolutely necessary to cover yourself in case your earning ability is cut through reasons such as illness/accident, death or being called to jury service. It is particularly important to protect yourself if you have dependants or wish to protect assets for inheritance purposes.

Investment

While protection is an essential requirement, investment is, in the strictest sense, a luxury. If you had to live on a state pension in the United Kingdom, you could, even if that was not what you had in mind when you started off as a consultant!

When you are setting up your consultancy, it is probably best to wait until you are well under way and the cash flow looks healthy before you start investing. The main types of insurance include:

- Life assurance.
- Personal accident or sickness; this will cover accidental death, permanent and temporary disablement.
- Loss or damage to contents of office.
- Jury service.
- Employers liability.
- Public liability.
- Professional liability.
- Consequential loss insurance. } for
- Products liability. } manufacturing
- Dread disease.

Most of the above categories will be familiar to you but the one area which is growing in importance for consultants is that of professional liability and indemnity insurance. For this reason, I have included, in Appendix 1, full details of this subject. In order that you may have a broad idea of the area covered, the following summary will show you whether you need to go into the subject in greater detail.

Summary of professional liability and indemnity insurance

As a consultant, you have a professional responsibility towards your clients. This includes being competent and, in some cases, holding a recognized qualification before you can offer a service. The public has an expectation of what level of competence and skills are necessary for you to practise in the area in which you profess expertise.

There is a degree of risk involved in each work opportunity and this is the liability you carry as a consultant. The risks need to be identified and then managed, and any part of the risk which is beyond your control should be transferred to an insurer.

Until about twenty years ago, most consultants did not seriously consider the risk of being sued. Now, more cases involving consultants are being brought to court. The consuming public is becoming increasingly aware of its rights and is less likely to accept careless or negligent behaviour on the part of those who offer services. As society becomes litigious, the body of law becomes broader and more complex. Traditional terms of agreement between consultant and client may not be sufficient to cover the consultant if the client brings an action for breach of contract because of a perceived failure to exercise the standard of professional skill which is implied in that contract. As the emerging professions, such as management or computer consultants, are not generally as strictly regulated or monitored as the more traditional professions, there is obviously scope for disagreement and misunderstanding.

If responsibilities and liabilities are clearly established between client and consultant, the surest way of guarding against any future loss and limiting its effect is through insurance. Details of professional indemnity insurance and other ways of reducing liability are given in Appendix 1. Your professional body will probably have considered the whole question of indemnity insurance. You should find out whether your sphere of operation is likely to leave you open to risk of legal action and take the appropriate steps. Certainly, those consultants whose work involves an element of physical danger, such as outdoor development activities, or those who include psychometric testing should seriously study what is on offer by the brokers. All consultants should at least think about their position in relation to their professional liability and indemnity insurance.

General advice on insurance

Never tie yourself to one provider. A reputable broker will be able to advise you on the suitability of the many policies on offer and will also let you know if regulations change. Keep talking to your adviser so that a good working relationship is built up and your portfolio is regularly updated. Do not be afraid to ask questions. Keep asking, until you fully understand what you are committing yourself to and you are happy that you have as full a cover for yourself and your business as is necessary.

Other consultants

Most independent consultants are part of a network and are quite used to answering questions about what they do, what they have achieved and how they got there. Some associations and other groups which include consultants run workshops or seminars in which they discuss best practice for new and would-be consultants.

If you are serious about being a consultant, you will probably have met others who are already working in the field and you will have decided which ones you wish to emulate. Ask them about what they have learned since they started up and what are the pitfalls facing the new consultant. By talking to other independent operators, you will soon find out which consultants are held in high regard by their peers.

Professional body

You may already belong to professional body or to an association whose members share your interests. It is useful to contact these bodies to see if they have a Code of Conduct or a statement of what they consider to be acceptable practice within their area of operation.

Designers

The designers used most often by consultants are those who are concerned with corporate identity, which includes letterheads, business cards and other items of office stationery. They will also help with designing and printing brochures and any other item that projects your image to potential clients.

Personnel

If you are going to employ other people, you may need some help in recruiting staff and keeping them. Someone involved in employment law will advise you on the wording of advertisements (particularly with reference to equal opportunities legislation), employee benefits, grievance procedures, contracts of employment and all aspects of being an employer.

Travel

If you are going to be involved in a substantial amount of business travelling it is worth identifying someone who can relieve you of the time-consuming task of making the travel arrangements. Some travel agencies have special departments dealing with business travel and are used to problems such as getting visas at short notice, advising on vaccinations and arranging limousine service if necessary. If accounts are sufficiently large, agencies may well offer some free travel or reduced rates during the year.

Health

The importance of remaining healthy is paramount. If you are self-employed, it is not always enough to have the necessary insurances should you fall ill. Should you have to cancel an assignment through ill health, not only will you lose money but you may lose credibility with the client, and that can mean no repeat business. In the worst instance, the client may sue you for 'consequential loss'. Have regular, comprehensive check-ups, not only with the doctor but also the dentist, optician and other specialists who can make sure that you are not succumbing to the stresses of the life you lead.

Many people also find it helpful to have access to other practitioners such as acupuncturists, masseurs and Alexander Technique teachers. We all subject our bodies to unnatural stresses during our everyday lives, for example, by the way we sit in our cars, in an aeroplane or at our desks, and it is useful to be able to deal with any physical discomfort brought about in these ways. This will also ease our mental condition and allow us to work at optimum capacity. (See Chapter 13 on health.)

5 Taxation

When you become self-employed, you will ask many questions about your tax position and other financial matters. The following chapter deals with some of the more common queries in the United Kingdom, but you should consult your own tax adviser on your specific position and the latest law relating to your situation and location.

What are the tax advantages and disadvantages of being a sole trader?

Advantages

- Expenses that can be claimed include a portion of some costs, i.e. phone, heat and light, and car expenses, that would probably be payable whether self-employed or not.
- The chance to work from home cuts out travelling time, but gives a greater opportunity to claim travel expenses which are incurred on journeys from your home base to most places. However, journeys from home to an office used as a base for business would not be allowable.
- A personal pension scheme may be arranged to suit your circumstances rather than a more structured company scheme. Allied to this is the ability to arrange a pension mortgage which is one of the most tax efficient methods of such finance.
- The basis of tax assessment can be very helpful to someone starting out, especially in the early years when profits tend to be

lower. If careful steps are taken the first accounting period profit can be used to measure three years tax assessments. For example, if the first accounts are drawn to 30 April 1992, that could be used to calculate Assessments for 1991/2, 1992/3 and 1993/4. Obviously, if this profit were £10,000 as against £15,000 and £20,000 for the following two years, there would be significant tax saving compared with paying on the profit arising within each tax year.

Disadvantages

- You have to rely mainly on your own resources to arrange tax in two instalments, half in January and half in July each year.
- Although not strictly tax – it feels the same – having Class 4 National Insurance contribution liability means it is collected along with Schedule D tax on business profits exceeding £5,050. This is levied at 6.3 per cent up to a profit of £16,900, giving a maximum payable of £746. Apart from allowing modest tax relief on this levy, it has no relevance in building up extra National Insurance benefits yet it is still lower than maximum contributions made by employed individuals. However, their contributions are supposed to give some potential benefits, such as unemployment benefit, which are not available to the self-employed.
- Sickness has to be coped with more heroically when you are self-employed; there is no employer to carry the pay burden, only basic National Insurance benefit. Although not strictly a tax point, it does show a need to obtain some sickness insurance. Regrettably, the cost of this cover is not tax deductible.

What are the tax advantages and disadvantages of being in a partnership?

Advantages

- These are similar to those for sole traders. When you join a partnership, you can arrange to give initial tax assessments which are much lower for the first year or two than the partners may have incurred as individuals.
- Although partners are *jointly* liable for the debts of a partnership, this does not extend to individual tax bills. The other people deeply involved in the business, namely the partners, are available

to give advice and support over difficult decisions and this is often extremely helpful.

Disadvantages

● Apart from it being more complicated to agree respective tax bills, there are no obvious tax disadvantages.

What are the tax advantages and disadvantages of being a limited company?

Advantages

● The liability to corporation tax with profits of up to £200,000 is restricted to 25 per cent. This means that if the owner is content to build up reserves within the company, a much lower tax is charged than if he takes a much larger personal salary. Although it is difficult to be specific because each individual's circumstances are different, it is usually worth forming into a company when profits exceed £45,000.

● Company pension schemes for 'owner directors' are far more generous in terms of tax relief than for an individual.

● Advantage may be taken of company car schemes, although clawback legislation tends to make these less advantageous.

● It is usually simpler to have wife/husband as director with accompanying pension/tax advantages than is the case with a person trading alone.

Disadvantages

● Annual returns have to be submitted to Company House and there are far more stringent audit requirements involved with a company than for a sole trader.

● If, after a few years, it is necessary to wind up the company and profits have been ploughed back to enjoy the lower company tax rate rather than take a higher salary, there can be a capital gains tax problem. This is because the effective value of the share will have increased with retained profits, giving a capital gain on disposal unless retirement relief is available.

When do I become eligible to pay VAT?

As soon as gross earnings/fees/turnover exceed £35,000 in the past year, you should register for value added tax (VAT). It is necessary to keep a monthly check, and local VAT offices, which are listed in the phone book, will help with registration and advise on records and returns.
Once you are registered, the *minimum* records should show clearly the gross income and VAT. It helps to show different categories of expense as well, so that not only VAT can be clearly related to specific items but also the records can also be used for income tax purposes later. You can only get credit for VAT paid with genuine invoices and every quarter Customs send a return on which is recorded VAT due for the quarter on earnings/turnover and VAT on business expenses. The difference shows either a net payment to Customs or they will credit any refund direct to your bank.
As VAT is run by HM Customs and Excise, not the Inland Revenue, they tend to be very strict and do not accept excuses. Once you are registered, you must take VAT seriously as their officers have draconian powers of entry to your property and access to your personal papers.

What about National Insurance contributions?

If you are self-employed, weekly National Insurance (NI) payments are due, and you can either buy stamps from a post office and stamp your own card or you arrange for the Department of Social Security (DSS) to direct debit every four weeks.
In addition, there are the Class 4 contributions mentioned earlier, which are collected together with the annual tax on profits. This levy is 6.3 per cent on profits between £5,050 and £16,900, with a maximum payable in 1989/90 of £746.

How are my tax commitments affected if I use my house as an office?

For both income tax and corporation tax, tax relief would be allowed on a fair proportion of all outgoings such as heat and light, repairs, and cleaning, relating to the property as a whole and to the office room(s) in particular.

The Inland Revenue may seek to claim on the house being sold, so that the proportion of a profit made similar to the 'business use' is treated under capital gains. However, if only a general claim is made under 'excess heat and light' and it is not claimed that the room is used *exclusively* for business, a reasonable claim can usually be agreed. The room can be used occasionally as a bedroom or homework room for children to get over the exclusive problem.

With the community charge, as with the old general rates, if a council thinks it can prove that a business is being run from home and it is disposed to push this point, it would be possible for it to assess that part of a house for business rates. This is a grey area, as different councils' policies vary. As a guide, if a taxi, hairdressing or timber business were run from home, and enough activity goes on so that neighbours become aware of it and complain to the council, there is more risk of being 'business rated' or prohibited from working at home than if the work means that just a few callers come to the house.

Accountant or taxation adviser – which do I use?

If you have a limited company, the accounts have to be audited and certified by a qualified or recognized accountant. Once that is done, it is quite acceptable for the tax liability to be agreed with the Inland Revenue by a tax adviser who does not need to be an accountant. Normally, however, the accountant will cover all the necessary work.

A tax advisor is normally used for preparing individual tax returns and agreeing annual tax liability with the Inland Revenue. It is quite normal for such a person to prepare and agree the annual statements of income and expenditure, as may be required for a sole trader, and the subsequent tax liability.

What records should I keep for tax purposes?

Ideally, you should keep a cash book which sets out on one side all income accruing to the business, with copy invoices where relevant, and on the other side all the expenses of the business. With expenses, there will probably be up to a dozen different sections in which to put various sub-headings so that expenses may be more accurately analysed. (See Figure 5.1.)

A specific business bank account should be used so that personal 'non-business' items are kept separate from your business accounts. At the end of the year, the bank statements and cheque book stubs will prove essential for a proper audit.

If you are registered for VAT, the same basic system can apply, with the addition of an extra column on both sides to record clearly VAT received on earnings and VAT paid and claimed on expenses, thus enabling recovery to be made. These need to be numbered and kept safely for seven years as the VAT inspectors will need to inspect them on a regular basis.

What is the difference between cash flow and profitability?

Most self-employed people and small businesses fail not because of a lack of profitability but because the cash did not flow at the appropriate times. You can have a theoretically profitable project – that is, the total amount of costs is exceeded by the price the client will pay – and still go bust! This is because the flows of money in and out are not synchronized. Either the client is slow in paying and/or you are too fast at paying your creditors. This is why it is essential to agree tough terms of business with your clients so that, if they do not pay on the due date, they will meet a significant financial penalty. You can be forced out of business for not paying a debt as low as £50, so it is necessary to monitor your cash flow very carefully.

Cash flow shows how much is coming into the business and how much is going out in any period. It is possible, for example, for income to increase substantially from £2000 to £8000 per month. Unless, however, expenses are kept within a reasonable proportion of income, the greater the amount of cash flowing in will not of itself increase profitability. If you have a business where expenses are kept at a level which does not move much but the income increases or decreases, then increased flow in terms of receipts would clearly tend to increase profitability. On the other hand, if it is a business which needs very large increases in expenses in order to create additional income, an increase in cash flow can exist alongside constant or even

Date	Invoice	Banked	Date	Travel/car (petrol, expenses, mainten- ance, etc)	Phones	Post & station- ery	Subs	Hotels & confer- ences	Bank charges	Journals & books	Materials	Insurance	Office expenses	Sundries	VAT Paid	Claimed

Figure 5.1 Example of headings used in cash book

Projected cash flows for the period January to June 1993

Month

CASH IN	£s	January	February	March	April	May	June	TOTALS
Midshire Corporation		–	2,000	9,000	–	–	1,000	12,000
Institute of Directors		1,000	–	1,000	1,000	1,000	–	4,000
British Chemicals		2,000	1,000	–	–	2,250	–	5,250
Super Trading		–	–	–	–	2,000	5,000	7,000
HK Radio		–	2,500	–	–	2,500	–	5,000
TOTAL IN		+3,000	+5,500	+10,000	+1,000	+7,750	+6,000	+33,250
CASH OUT								
Monthly outgoings		2,348	2,348	2,348	2,348	2,348	2,348	14,088
Plane tickets		–	–	3,100	–	–	1,550	4,650
Kuala Lumpur trip		–	–	–	780	–	–	780
House Insurance		–	–	986	–	–	–	986
Loan payback		–	–	1,000	–	–	1,000	2,000
Telephones		–	300	–	–	300	–	600
Professional subs		480	–	–	–	–	55	535
TOTAL OUT		–2,828	–2,648	–7,434	–3,128	–2,648	–4,953	–23,639
DIFFERENCE IN/OUT		+172	+2,852	+2,566	–2,128	+5,102	+1,047	+9,611
CUMULATIVE DIFFERENCE		–1,693	+1,159	+3,725	+1,597	+6,699	+7,746	
STARTING BALANCE								
–1,865								

Figure 5.2 A typical cash flow forecast

dropping profitability. One advantage of VAT registration is that it can give a quarterly exercise in checking the cash flow and profitability when the return is prepared. To that extent, if such reviews are not carried out, a year looking back can leave matters too late if there is a problem to be overcome. A typical cash flow is shown in Figure 5.2.

How do I set up a simple cash flow monitoring system?

If you do a simple chart over a twelve month period and show a graph line based on average monthly income of the previous year, this will show how much above or below the average each month has been. It is then sensible to project in pencil the next, say, one or two months, and then complete each month as it is finished. If, for example, the average monthly income (ignoring VAT) is £2,500, the picture as shown in Figure 5.3 would emerge. Expenses can be shown on a similar chart using the average monthly expenses of the previous year as the axis line.

It is important to know where to place the proprietor's drawings (that is, what he pays to himself). Many people think these are a

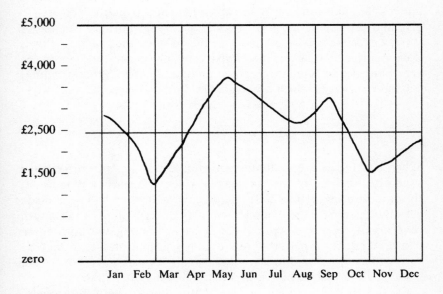

Figure 5.3 Cash-flow chart

business expense or an identifiable salary, but they are not. The taxable profit totally ignores drawings and you could have a position whereby profit is £27,000 and drawings only £16,000 but it is on the larger figure that tax is based. By drawing off less of the profit, the amount of cash retained in the business is greater. Similarly, if the profit is £20,000 and drawings are £36,000, the tax position is still based on £20,000. This situation just means that more has been taken out of the business than was earned in that year, which can be funded either by a surplus retained from the previous year or an increase in loan facilities. Whether or not the monthly drawings are included in the expenditure cash flow figures, remember that they are not a business expense as such, merely an 'advance on profits'.

How do I build up a profit and loss account and a balance sheet?

Usually the accountant will do this on an annual basis when she does the accounts, based on the books and records maintained under her advice. It is, however, sensible to keep a regular quarterly check and this could be done with reference to the VAT return. The last profit and loss account can simply be substituted by the quarter's figures to give the proprietor a good idea of where the business stands. A similar exercise can be adopted on the balance sheet and, if this is done quarter by quarter, it will give a regular check throughout the year until the accountant prepares the final figures. Some computer software packages which are available do these exercises very well.

When will I first be liable for tax?

When starting as a consultant, you should tell the Inland Revenue soon after the end of the tax year in which you start to practice. If the date was, say, 1 June 1991 and no communication had been made with the tax office, then mention should be made on your tax return covering the year to 5 April 1992. There is no obligation to prepare first accounts for a period of less than a year and, in fact, it may be decided to cover eighteen months to 31 December 1992 before preparing the first accounts, and then annually after that.

On the assumption that the Inland Revenue know of the income, they will probably issue estimated assessments on profit for the tax years 1991/2 and 1992/3 in the autumn of 1992. If these estimates are excessive, appeals have then to be lodged on your behalf, with a suggestion made as to a reasonable payment on account pending final figures being prepared and agreed.

Normally you would expect to pay something on account of 1991/2 tax by October/November 1992 and a further payment on account of the first instalment of 1992/3 tax in January 1992; and, if final figures are still not agreed by early summer 1993, a further payment on 1 July in respect of the second instalment of 1992/3 tax. Once figures are agreed, any extra tax – or a refund – can be arranged. Schedule D tax on profits is based on the agreed profit for the accounting year ended in the previous tax year. Once established, the profit to 31 December 1993 will be taxed in 1993/4 in two equal instalments due 1 January and 1 July 1994. There are special arrangements for the first couple of years, as indicated earlier.

What allowances can I claim?

Normally any expenditure laid out wholly and necessarily in respect of the business is allowable. Such headings include phone, subscriptions, fares, car expenses, books, magazines, postage, stationery, hotels, course fees, bank charges, rents and/or use of home as office, equipment repairs, etc. Obviously the list is fairly extensive but experience, advice and negotiations will determine a list applicable to each business.

Who has to know that I am self-employed?

- HM Inspector of Taxes in the area where your business is based.
- Local VAT office if gross earnings exceed £35,000 (or whatever the annual limit may be set at).
- Your bank will certainly be interested to know, even if you do not use them for credit purposes. It is always useful to keep the bank in the picture. If finance is not required immediately, it is an unusual business that does not need help occasionally.
- Check things like car and house insurance, as there are sometimes restrictions or extra loadings for being self-employed.
- Should you need to alter premises (or use your home) to

accommodate the business, planning permission may be required. If you are simply using a room at home without upsetting neighbours or local facilities, then unofficial enquiries may be sensible with the local authority rather than a specific approach. There is no need to expose yourself to business rating if the council is one of many that are unlikely to impose it. It can be expensive being totally open when 'unofficially' the council usually ignores this type of limited use.

If I employ anyone, will I have to deduct income tax?

Unless the employee earns under £2,500 p.a. with *no* outside earnings, PAYE will have to operated. Employees have the duty to arrange their own coding and the Inland Revenue will give you a set of tax and NI tables to consult in your capacity as an employer. From these you have to calculate the correct deduction from each employee's weekly or monthly gross pay for tax and NI, according to the codes applicable. The employer has to pay over the amounts deducted for tax and NI to the Collector of Taxes on a monthly or quarterly basis. If there is no coding for an employee, you will have to apply 'Emergency Coding' against pay until a proper coding is arranged. It is illegal for you to work out the coding for an employee even if you are able to do so; the coding must come from the Inland Revenue. Obviously, there are heavy penalties for not conforming to the regulations, especially not paying money over once deducted.

Do the same rules apply if I use a sub-contractor on an assignment?

When a person works for you on a specific short-term assignment, and cannot be said to be a direct employee, all you need to do is pay that person's fees and the cost to you will be a business expense in the usual way. There should be no necessity for you to operate PAYE for that person.

As a wife, am I treated differently for tax purposes?

The simple answer is 'No', as from 6 April 1990. From this date, each individual will be treated separately. Previously, a wife's income had to be disclosed on her husband's tax return, although she has been (and will continue to be) responsible for maintaining all normal records for a business operated by her personally.

What is the difference between tax avoidance and tax evasion, and what is legitimate?

Tax avoidance is legal. It covers specific actions designed to reduce your personal tax bill; for example, pension schemes, mortgage, and business expansion schemes. Someone who is domiciled abroad and who has large investment income overseas can avoid UK tax simply by not remitting it.

On the other hand, evasion is hiding income from the Inland Revenue by, for example, working for cash and never disclosing the income. Similarly, claiming expenses, – fictitious, excessive, or obviously not business-related – in accounts can be classed as falsely obtaining tax relief.

How is my tax position affected if I decide to wind up the consultancy?

At the start of a business, the advantages are with the taxpayer, whereas on ceasing a business, the advantages are with the Inland Revenue. Under Schedule D rules, the normal basis of assessment is the profit received in the previous tax year. On winding up, however, the Inland Revenue has the right to adjust the tax assessments on the two final full tax years if the result gives them more tax. However, they can only adjust both years or neither – they cannot choose only one. As a result, it is sensible to take advice as to which date (assuming there is a choice) to finish. Normally, with an increasing trend of profit, it is better to cease soon after 5 April, but with a decreasing profit, it is best to cease before 5 April. This is a difficult matter to explain, and it is best to seek advice when the situation is likely to arise.

What are the penalties?

Not registering for VAT, not submitting regular accounts, or not paying NI contributions are all offences, and could expose you to legal action by the authorities. It is more likely, however, that, once the failure is known to have occurred, a financial penalty will be levied.

- For VAT this is up to 20 per cent of the net VAT due on earnings, less expenses for the period the failure has existed. In addition, all VAT has to be paid retrospectively whether it can be recovered from customers or not, which could bring instant bankruptcy if a sufficient sum is involved. If the delay in registration is two years, it is almost certain to give rise to a penalty of 20 per cent of the net VAT due to be paid for the period from when registration should have taken place. The penalty increases from 10 per cent to 30 per cent depending on the delay in registering.

- For income tax, the possible penalties are too complex to detail but failure to submit a tax return with accounts within six months of the end of the tax year can bring a £300 penalty plus £60 a day once the failure has been noticed and continues. In practice, this would only normally be used if a new source of income or business had arisen. Any penalty for negligence or fraud in a tax return or accounts can be equal to the tax lost plus interest at commercial rates, from the date the tax should have been paid.

- With National Insurance, when the mistake/oversight is notified by the individual, experience suggests that the DSS is usually content to collect the back contribution. Obviously, if the department finds the failure and it is for a long period – probably more than two years – then legal action may well be taken, but, again, possible penalty provisions are too extensive to list.

6 The Written Word

Many people feel uncomfortable with the written word. They put off writing reports and proposals and they dash off poorly conceived letters because they have not been taught to write in a way that is useful at work. The value of logically constructed, accurate, comprehensible and interesting written communication is considerable. If you realize that this is not one of your strengths, this section will help you feel more confident about putting pen to paper (or fingers to keyboard).

The general rules about writing are the same regardless of the type of document you are producing, so it may be helpful to look at those rules first and follow up with a discussion of the different forms the writing may take. Written communications should be clear, readable, relevant and informative. To achieve this, the following guidelines should be observed:

Language

The written word in business should be simple and straightforward. Writers often think that reports and letters have to be written in a different language from the spoken word, but this usually leads to complex sentences and the misuse of words. If you have any problems writing a sentence or paragraph, try saying it out loud. This usually helps to clarify your thoughts.

Although you should always be aware of the person who will be reading what you write, and so use the appropriate words and way of presenting the material, you do not have to use a different kind of English for each type of reader. Your aim is clarity. You are not trying to bewilder or mystify the reader or to make life difficult for yourself.

Be clear

Do not allow room for ambiguity or wrong assumptions. For example, the following sentence could have two meanings: 'The MD told the accountant that he had made a mistake.'

Keep it short and simple (KISS)

As an author, you are aiming at clarity of expression, balance of ideas and arguments, and interest in what has been written. You should, therefore, keep sentences and paragraphs short and simple. It is advisable to break long sentences down into shorter ones to avoid overusing punctuation. As a sentence grows in length, the rate of reading and comprehension slows down.

Do not use many words when a few will do, or complicated phrases to express a simple idea. For example: in the event that/if; we are in a position to undertake/we can; endeavour to ascertain/try to find out.

It is generally easier to read statements using the active voice rather than the passive voice. It is usually shorter, too. For example: it was declared by John that/John said; the undersigned was not telephoned by your assistant/your assistant did not phone me.

Keep jargon in its place

You may be able to use technical words for some readers but you may have to explain them to others. Do not resort to jargon unless it is appropriate to the audience. Generally, your technical words and phrases will be incomprehensible to a lay audience.

Avoid clichés

For example: 'at this moment in time', the general standard of

English 'leaves much to be desired', but 'it goes without saying' that, 'at the end of the day', it will 'all come out in the wash'.

Use punctuation to help the reader

Punctuation does for writing what pauses do for speech. It is often better to break long sentences down into shorter ones than to worry about whether to use brackets or dashes.

The importance of punctuation is shown in the following examples which use the same words but mean completely different things:

- The photocopiers, which have been given new drums, are now working properly.
- The photocopiers which have been given new drums are now working properly.

The use of correct English

There are still some of us old-fashioned enough to believe that there are right and wrong ways of writing English. Unfortunately, many people have not had the benefit of learning the rules. Consequently, by the time they come to study and work, they do not feel at ease with the demands of producing the wide range of written documents required of them.

There are many potential traps for authors and there are some useful books on the market (see Recommended Reading). In this book, it is not possible to cover all the pitfalls but I shall mention a few.

Spelling

There are those who can and those who can't! If you have a spell check on your word processor, make sure that it is appropriate for your work; that is, does it have English or American spelling? The dictionary is an invaluable aid and, together with a thesaurus, should always be at hand. Some people are fortunate enough to have their work typed by someone who can spell, but these paragons seem to be in increasingly short supply.

Commonly misspelt words include the following:

- necessary
- separate
- definite
- correspondence
- liaison
- accommodation
- occasion

All these have to be learnt by heart, unless you have developed any little tricks to remember them. Examples of this would be to remember that: the word 'finite' is part of 'definite', not 'finate' which does not exist; in 'necessary', the sequence of 'c' and 's' is 1–2; and the two 'i's' ('eyes') in 'liaison' help you make the connection.

'Couples'

There are some 'couples' of words which cause confusion. They include:

- principle/principal
- practise/practice
- stationery/stationary
- dependent/dependant
- complement/compliment

Do you know the difference between them in all cases? If you would like to check, you will find explanations and examples at the end of the chapter.

Similar words

There are other pairs of words which are similar in sound or spelling but which have distinct meanings. They include:

- practical/practicable
- disinterested/uninterested
- continual/continuous
- effect/affect

Are you sure when each of these should be used? Again, there are examples at the end of the chapter.

Word endings

It is sometimes difficult to remember how words change when -ed or -ing are added. For example:

● benefit	benefited	benefiting
● commitment	committed	committing
● focus	focused	focusing
● fulfil	fulfilled	fulfilling

'All right' and 'alright'

- *All right* is correct.
- *Alright* is always wrong.

Apostrophes

- They should not be used to indicate a plural as in 'hot drink's served here' or 'hundreds of jobs for temp's'.
- 'It's' means 'it is' – the apostrophe shows that something has been left out.
- 'Its' shows possession.
- We have dealt with our client's/clients' problems for many years. Client's: the problems of our client. Clients': the problems of our clients.

Fewer and less

There are dozens of examples of the incorrect use of these two words on the radio and television every day. 'Less' refers to mass, volume, extent or quantity, where it is difficult to be exact about numbers. For example: 'there is less choice in this shop'. 'Fewer' is more specific and refers to numbers. 'there were fewer choices in the exam questions this year'.

This chapter has dealt with only a few of the challenges facing an author. Some of the books mentioned in the 'Recommended reading' will be particularly useful for those who would like help in this area. Your professional institute may offer appropriate training, and there are many public courses available. Remember; there is no shame in admitting that you find writing difficult. Be honest with yourself and spend some time confronting the problem and practising the skill.

Explanations and examples

'Couples' (see page 54)

1 *Principle*   is a noun and means 'fundamental belief or truth', 'general law', or 'code of right conduct'. For example: 'the machine works on the principle that . . .' and 'we agreed in principle to go ahead with the scheme'.

   Principal   may be a noun, meaning 'person in charge' or an adjective meaning 'main' or 'chief'. For example: 'My principal reason for seeing you is . . .' and 'Mrs Green is the college's Principal'. (Remember make a *pal* of the Principal!)

2 *Practise*   is a verb.
   Practice   is a noun.
    For example: 'The medical practice has six doctors' and 'practice makes perfect'; but 'I have been practising my pronunciation'.

    Similar pairs are: license/licence
                         devise/device
                         prophesy/prophecy
                         advice/advise

    It often helps to think of 'advise' and 'advice' if you have difficulty with the others.

3 *Stationery*   is a noun and means 'office materials'. For example: 'I went to the stationery cupboard for paper, pens and staples'. (Remember: 'e' stands for 'envelopes'!)

   Stationary   is an adjective meaning 'not moving'. For example: 'The car was stationary outside the house during the night'.

4 *Dependent*   has an adjectival use. For example: 'my mother is dependent on me for financial support since her accident'.

   Dependant   means a person who depends on another for

support. For example: 'you may be able to claim some tax relief as you support your dependants'.

5 *Complement* means 'to make whole'. For example: 'this car has its full complement of passengers' and 'the present shopping centre will be complemented by a sports hall'.

Compliment is 'to praise'. For example: 'we complimented her on the well-written report'.

Similar words *(see page 54)*

1 *Practical* contrasts with 'theoretical' and means 'useful'. For example: 'the emphasis of the course was on practical demonstrations rather than on theoretical ideas'.

Practicable means capable of being put into practice, 'workable'. For example: 'it was not practicable to invite all their friends to the small flat'.

2 *Disinterested* means 'impartial'. For example: 'judges and football referees should be 'disinterested'.

Uninterested means 'not interested', 'doesn't care'. For example: 'the atheist is uninterested in religion'.

3 *Continuous* means 'uninterrupted', 'an unbroken sequence'.

Continual Frequent, referring to something that happens repeatedly but not constantly. For example: 'water may flow continuously' but a tap drips 'continually'.

4 *Effect* can be either a verb or a noun and means 'to bring about', 'accomplish'. For example: to give up smoking may 'effect' an improvement in your health; or smoking may have 'an effect' on your health.

Affect is a verb and means 'to have an effect on'. For example: smoking may 'affect' your health.

7 Letters

As a consultant, you will have to write letters and for most people it takes practice to make it a task that you do not face with annoyance and despondency. Even if you do not have a natural flair for the written word, follow a few simple rules and your letters will be clear and present a good image of you and the work you do.

Prepare thoroughly

- Make sure that you are addressing the recipient of the letter in the correct way, or the way which he prefers.
- Collect together the necessary support material, such as previous correspondence and relevant files, so you have to hand all the facts you need.
- Note down what you need to say in a logical order. At first, you may have to write down most of the letter but, as you become more confident, you will manage with a list of headings to remind you of what you want to say.
- Research the extra information you need such as unusual spellings of names, places or products, references, enclosures and extra copies. Also consider how you will address the recipient. Is he 'Dear Sir'; 'Dear Mr Jackson', 'Dear David' or 'My dear Dave'? The salutation may set the tone for the rest of the letter.

You are now ready to write the letter, or to dictate it to a shorthand writer or into an audio machine.

Identify the subject

The easiest way of referring to the reason for writing is to have a heading at the beginning of the body of the letter, as in the following example:

27 October 1990

Mr David Jackson
Training and Development Manager
C B Allspice plc
124 Crabtree Street
London SE1 9PW

Dear David

Strategy workshop – preliminary discussion

Thank you for your letter of 24 October 1990 in which you expressed an interest in talking to me about staging a strategy workshop for your board of directors.

State the facts

If you have been in contact with the recipient before, it will be useful to summarize what has gone before. This is particularly important if there is any chance of misunderstanding, so that any potential problems may be identified quickly. You must be sure that your facts are accurate and that you present them clearly and concisely.

As you reminded me, you contacted me following the seminar I ran at the Institute of Human Resources where you were a participant and played such an active role.

You will be aware, I am sure, that a workshop for your directors would be substantially different from the seminar as the activity would be specially designed for your organization's needs.

Show the way ahead

This is where you let the recipient know what action needs to be taken and who will be responsible for it.

> We shall obviously need to have a preliminary meeting to discuss your needs and my approach to such a workshop, and I should be delighted to come to your offices if that is most acceptable to you.
>
> I shall telephone your secretary in the next few days to arrange a mutually convenient time for our meeting.

Conclusion

You should end your letters with simple, polite statements which leave the reader feeling positive and not left hanging in mid-air.

> I am most grateful for your interest in my work and hope that we may co-operate in this venture.
>
> I look forward to meeting you again soon.
>
> Yours sincerely
>
> Margaret Ensign

When you read through the finished letter, you should feel happy that it has set the right tone and is consistent with your relationship with the recipient. It should not be too familiar or too abrupt and, as well as covering all the facts, it should be interesting and easy to read.

8 Proposals

While all proposals contain the same basic information, the format will vary according to the situation. For example, it is easier to give specific details of content and timing for a training course than for a development activity. Indeed, many consultants write proposals which are not selling documents, but rather a written confirmation of what has been agreed with the client during discussions.

A proposal is usually a selling document when the consultant is responding to a request to quote for a specific activity, often in competition against other consultants. In most cases the consultant will have been contacted before the request is received to make sure that she is interested in principle in being considered for the work. The request for you to submit a proposal may be in the form of a document with all the relevant details spelled out, which will be considered sufficient for you to draw up a proposal. You may have to supply further details of yourself, your qualifications and experience and, in some cases, references to support your claim that you are able to carry out the work. As a general rule, requests from the public sector will be more formal than those from the private sector and the amount of supporting paperwork correspondingly greater.

Where a project has been discussed at length between client and consultant, the proposal serves only to ensure that each party understands what has been said and agreed, as all the groundwork will have been covered already.

Occasionally, as part of a marketing ploy, a consultant may send

64

an unsolicited proposal to a company, having identified some needs within that organization which she feels able to meet. This, and other marketing techniques, will be discussed in Chapter 7.

A proposal, whether used as a selling document or a confirmation, must contain the following information (although often a formal request will have its own design and headings for you to follow):

- terms of reference
- method and content of consultancy
- consultant(s) involved
- timing of project
- breakdown of costs
- terms of business

If the consultant sends a second copy of the proposal for the client to sign, providing it is acceptable, and return to the consultant, then usually a contract is not needed as well.

Example of a simple proposal

BRAITHWAITE, SCUTTLE AND BLOWES

Course Proposal

REPORT WRITING

Context

On 26 January 1991, Terry Scuttle, Senior Partner of Braithwaite, Scuttle and Blowes, and Isobel Wilson, Communications Consultant, met to discuss a possible course on report writing for approximately sixteen members of staff from the Bradford office of BSB.

As the demands on partners' time increase, there is a need to delegate specific tasks, including report writing, to other people. In order that high standards of both content and presentation may be set and maintained and so that a uniform house style may be agreed, it is proposed to run a programme to provide delegates with the necessary skills and confidence to produce high quality reports with the minimum of anxiety and time-wasting.

This proposal contains a brief outline of the content of the programme and a quotation for developing and running the activity. It will provide the basis for discussion on the final format.

Aims and objectives

It is the aim of the programme to provide the delegates with the opportunity to:

(a) agree a common format for reports, and
(b) draw up a step-by-step approach to report writing which will make clear presentation easier and save the time of both writer and reader.

Method and format

(a) As approximately sixteen people are involved, it is proposed to work with them in two groups of eight. This will ensure maximum participation and enable everyone to make a full contribution.

(b) The first stage of the programme will be a half-day session with the seven partners to agree a common format for reports. Isobel Wilson will act as a facilitator during this activity and will record all the issues discussed and the format proposed.

(c) The second stage will be a one-day session with each group and will introduce the agreed house style and report format and then look at the basics of report writing.

Isobel Wilson will act as tutor, with formal input, as appropriate, to introduce and reinforce salient points, but participants will be expected to contribute fully to discussions. There will be short writing exercises, and delegates will be asked to bring along a report they have written or examples of good and bad writing so that they may assess them in the light of the guidelines.

(d) Comprehensive handouts will be provided so that each participant will be able to build up a useful set of notes and reference material.

Programme development

It is recommended that the tutor spends a short time with the

66

partners before the programme to ensure that she positions the activity in the most appropriate way.

Facilitator and tutor

A CV for Isobel Wilson is attached.

Timetable

This has to be finalized. Isobel Wilson will be available between 18 April and 27 April 1990.

Accommodation

To be decided by BSB and will preferably be away from the BSB offices.

Equipment required

Flip charts and markers
Overhead projectors and transparencies.

Costs

Facilitator's fee for:

(a)	Programme development (pre-programme discussions, preparation of material, and administration)	£ 600.00
(b)	Stage One 1 × ½ day session	300.00
(c)	Stage Two 2 × 1-day sessions	1200.00
	Total	£2100.00

Expenses for:

(a) Any travel, hotel and subsistence expenses incurred during this project will be charged at cost. Unless otherwise agreed, rail travel will be First Class and air travel will be Business Class. Mileage is charged at 30p per mile.

(b) Reprographic, photographic, graphic, courier and other reasonable expenses directly related to the project will be charged at
cost.

Invoicing

An invoice will be submitted on completion of the project. Payment
is due within thirty days of the invoice date and interest will be
charged at five per cent compound per month if payment is not
received by the due date.

Cancellation and postponement

In case of the programme being cancelled or postponed, the following scale of charges will be applied:

(a) more than six weeks' notice   no charge
(b) between four and six weeks' notice   50%
(c) between two and four weeks' notice   75%
(d) less than two weeks' notice   full charge

Expenses already incurred will be charged in addition.

Valid until 31 December 1991

Isobel Wilson
February 1991

For a simple proposal, the above example may seem rather long!
I have included many of the items that could also be part of a
contract. However, this document would spare you the effort of
having to write an additional contract if the client agreed to the
proposal, either by signing a copy or sending a letter confirming that
it was acceptable. Contracts are covered in more detail in Chapter 10.

Terms of business may be enclosed on a separate document. These
include expenses, payment of invoices, cancellation and postponement. For more details, see Chapter 10.

While the above example covers many of the relevant items in a
proposal, you may need to include others or expand on those

mentioned. For example, on a long or complicated project, you may wish to include a project schedule rather than a simple statement of when the activity will take place. In this case, some visual illustration, such as a bar chart or flow diagram, would assist the client. Also, if the project is designed to last over a long period, you may wish to build in monitoring mechanisms or progress reports. A schedule for these, possibly linked to payment of interim invoices, would be helpful here.

If you intend to use other people on the project, you should let the client know and include CVs of other consultants and details of sub-contractors. The client should be clear about the lines of responsibility, that is, who is dealing with who, so that there is no danger of misunderstanding.

On some projects, the client may require progress reports, final reports and other documentation, and the proposal should make it clear what this additional material will be.

Finally, if the consultant is to report to any working groups or committees within the client organization, the roles and responsibilities of everyone involved should be clearly defined.

9 Reports

Consultants may be asked to write reports at any stage of an assignment, or none at all. A feasibility study may be requested, either before a client makes a final choice between consultants or to help the client decide whether or not to go ahead with the project. During a lengthy project, various interim or progress reports may have to be submitted, and the most likely report will be the one written at the end of the assignment. Other documents, such as proposals, may come under the broad heading of reports.

A report is an extremely important document. It may be the basis by which you are judged and on which the success or otherwise of the project is measured, so it is obviously in your interest to make sure that it conveys what you want it to, in the clearest and most appropriate way.

The following section will look first at the format of reports, that is, the component parts and what they should cover, and secondly, at preparing and producing a report. If you have not had complete responsibility for producing reports in the past, your first solo attempt may seem quite daunting. That is why I have gone into detail in this section. Even if you are used to writing reports, you might find it helpful to use this section as a refresher course, and possibly a source of new ideas.

Format of report

Parts of a report

The following list covers most of the headings that you will need to consider when writing a report. Some will apply to nearly all reports and others may not be used at all in your particular field. The order may vary slightly; for example, a glossary may come early on if the writer feels it is essential for the reader to look at it before he moves on to the main part of the report.

Parts of report	Comments
● Cover page	Preferably high quality
● Disclaimer letter	If appropriate
● Title page	Same as cover page
● Contents	List titles of sections and page numbers
● Executive summary	If appropriate
● Statement of qualifications	If appropriate
● Acknowledgements	If appropriate
● Terms of reference/ Introduction	Sets the context
● Procedure	If such detail is appropriate (may be included in disclaimer)
● Findings	The main body of the report. This may
● Discussion/analysis/ arguments	be in separate sections or included together under sections covering the most
● Conclusions	important aspects of the investigation
● Recommendations	
● Appendices	Supplementary material
● Bibliography	Other useful background reading
● References	Books, journals, and so on, mentioned in the report
● Glossary	List of symbols, definitions, abbreviations, and so on.

Cover page

● The cover page gives the reader the initial information about the report's content and conveys the first impressions of the writer.

● A typical cover page may look like this:

Taylor and Cox
Consultants

NEWCOMBE, GIBSON AND ASHE

**Report on Provision of New Computer
System at Wimbledon Site**

Volume 1

October 1990

Disclaimer

A disclaimer usually takes the form of a letter and may be used by, for example, financial consultants who have been asked to make a financial review and need to make the boundaries of their investigation absolutely clear. In such a case, it may run as follows:

> We would point out that the procedures and enquiries do not constitute an audit. We are, therefore, unable to express any opinion on the financial statements of the company or on any other financial data referred to or included in our report.

As the awareness of 'intellectual property' grows (see Chapter 14), it becomes increasingly important to cover yourself in this area, and so a paragraph may be included in the disclaimer letter as follows:

> The enclosed report is for the sole information of Nelson, Barter and Company Limited, and is not to be otherwise referred to, in whole or in part, or quoted by excerpt or reference in any manner, or distributed to any third party without our written consent.

Title page

The title page looks like the cover but is printed on plain paper without your logo or letter heading. If there is no disclaimer, the title page may double as the cover page. In this case, you should protect the title page with a clear plastic sheet, perhaps showing your logo.

Executive summary

This summary is a brief overview of the key points and conclusions raised in the report and is written when the main report is completed. It enables the reader to find out quickly what the report is about before committing the time to reading the full document.

Contents

A typical contents page is shown below:

Acknowledgements

Acknowledge any help, advice and sources of information contained in the report. First, that is normal courtesy, but there are other reasons. With growing awareness of 'intellectual property' rights (see Chapter 14), it is wise to acknowledge your use of other people's material. Also, your own reputation will be enhanced if you are generous in your recognition of other people's contributions and achievements.

Terms of reference/introduction

This section states why the report was written and for whom. It sets the context. Within this section you will mention, as appropriate, the situation when you started the project, the scope of the survey, the timetable, the people involved, and any other information that will enable the reader to feel confident that all relevant aspects of the investigation have been taken into account.

Procedure

This section may have been included in the Introduction or put in the disclaimer letter. However, some people like to describe the method of enquiry and sources used in a separate section.

Findings, discussion/analysis/argument, conclusions and recommendations

The main body of the report, and its length and complexity will determine whether the different parts are handled under the same heading or as separate items.

The findings will result from the discussion, analysis and argument which, in turn, will lead to the conclusions – the issues that have been identified. The recommendations suggest what should happen as a result of the report in order to resolve the problems and to fulfill the report's purpose.

Appendices

An Appendix should amplify information referred to in the main body of the report. It prevents too much detail obscuring the main arguments of the report and follows on from the body of report.

Some people refer to 'exhibits' in reports. These are used to provide examples or to illustrate specific points within the main body of the report. Exhibits are usually boxed for easy reference and legibility.

References

If the writer has referred to any books, journals, articles, and so on, during the report, details should be listed here.

Bibliography

In addition to the supplementary material provided in the appendices, the writer may wish to include a list of other useful background reading material.

Glossary

A glossary may not be necessary if the report is to be read only by people fully conversant with the subject's specialist vocabulary. If the report is to be circulated to a more general readership, then a list of symbols, definitions, and abbreviations would be most helpful.

Preparing a report

In order to save time and to make report writing a pleasure rather than a chore, you must follow some simple rules.

Define the purpose of the report

Make sure you know *why* you are writing the report and for whom. It is then easier to decide how the report shall be produced.

Check: is the aim of the report

- to describe?
- to explain?
- to instruct?
- to persuade?
- to protest?
- to evaluate and recommend?
- to provoke debate?
- to record?
- something else?

Analyse the subject and identify the main topics

If you are writing a report which is similar to others you have produced, it is easy to make assumptions about the content and to become complacent if the subject is familiar. Each time you start preparing a report, check that you feel comfortable about what is important for this particular document and also understand what is irrelevant.

Using a spider diagram, mind map or one of the brainstorming techniques may help you clarify key areas at this stage. These are explained in greater detail on pages 77–80.

Collect available and relevant data

This stage may take a considerable time as the amount of data available may seem endless or non-existent. It is vital, therefore, to:

● decide what you need
● find out where to get the data
● get the data
● make sure the data is accurate

Sort the data and select relevant information

Look through the data you have collected and arrange it in a logical order. Review what you have collected to make sure it is relevant, always bearing in mind the purpose of the report.

Decide if the material is:

● for the main body of the report
● supplementary material
● possibly not relevant but may be considered later.

Examine and prepare the information for presentation

You may have the information in many different forms – articles, interview notes, other reports and so on. You may have to redraw or compile graphs or tables, précis or rewrite other written material before it is ready for inclusion in the report. Check details thoroughly at this stage since this will save time later. This stage of preparation may take a long time but will make it easier to write the report subsequently.

Write the report

As you will now have all the information gathered together in a logical order, it should not take long to write the report. You will now be concerned with the style and tone of the writing, which have been covered in Chapter 6.

Producing the final report

The first draft gives the author a chance to amend, delete or add material as appropriate or, if necessary, to alter the shape of the report. The final stages are now as follows.

Typing, copying and binding

Make sure you have given yourself enough time to get the report typed. Liaise with the person who will do the typing to make sure she is properly briefed and has the time to deal with all subsequent drafts before the final version is ready. If you have to do all the typing yourself, then obviously you will need to schedule the work carefully, making sure that you have sufficient supplies of the necessary stationery and that you will not run out of toner for the copier.

Also check that there is time to photocopy or print the report, as well as binding it before distribution.

Revision

Revision is essential if the report is to be worthy of the work put into the assignment. As you revise the draft, bear the following points in mind and, if possible, ask someone else to double-check them:

- does this report say what I want it to say?
- have I said it in the best possible way?
- is everything there?
- does it look good?

Final check

Check the typescript for errors. If possible, leave it for a day as it will be easier to spot mistakes after a break. Errors in a report give an impression of carelessness and may destroy the reader's confidence in your ability.

Stay alert during your proof-reading or serious mistakes may well slip through. For example, 'the suppliers are *now* ready to deliver the computers' may have been typed instead of 'the suppliers are *not* ready to deliver the computers', and there is, of course, a world of difference between the two statements even though they both make sense. It is also worth checking line-endings, as word divisions like 'the-rapist' interrupt the flow of reading and concentration.

Check details like numbering and sequence, as well as reading to ensure that the report makes sense. Check for consistency throughout the report in the use of technical language, companies' and peoples names, and the way abbreviations (BBC or B.B.C.) and dates (19 October 1990 or 19th October, 1990) are typed.

Now the report is ready for copying and distribution.

Brainstorming techniques

A number of techniques are available to help authors record ideas and issues in a different way from the traditional list. Two of them are shown here. Although they are similar in many ways, people usually find that one method is easier to use than the others. Do not worry if you have difficulty in working with either of these techniques. Some people do not like them and prefer more conventional approaches, using them to great effect.

Mind maps or brain patterns

Tony Buzan has described this process of codifying ideas in his excellent book *Use Your Head*. It enables your mind to be as free as possible in recording ideas, so that it is easy to add new thoughts as they occur. Related ideas may be circled or connected, perhaps using different colours, when the exercise is completed. We are used to working from the top left-hand side of a piece of paper but the world around us is not so tidy and an apparently random recording of data becomes easy after practice. The theme is written down in the centre of a sheet of paper and all the different subject areas branch out from the main idea. (See Figure 9.1.)

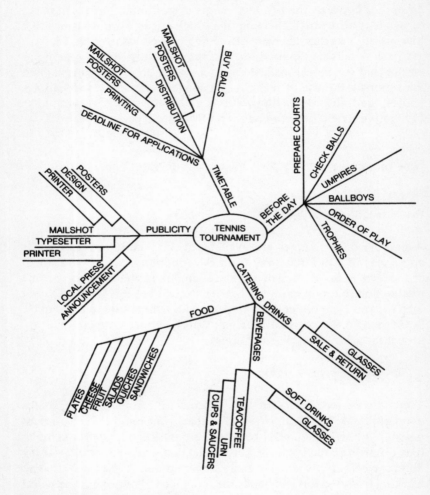

Figure 9.1   A mind map

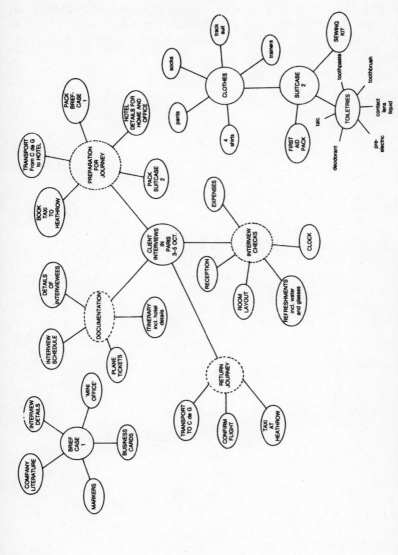

Figure 9.2 A spider diagram for a short overseas trip

Spider diagram

A spider diagram is also based on the brain pattern but looks slightly different. The main subject of the report is written in a 'bubble' on the page, and all other ideas, represented by a key word or phase, are also enclosed in 'bubbles', to be connected later by lines. (See Figure 9.2.)

10 The Practice

If only consultancy consisted merely of working with clients on projects! Being an independent operator, though, entails a great many other activities. This chapter examines the practical aspects of your operation.

It is almost impossible not to become involved with every aspect of running a practice, especially at the beginning. All the messages management consultants give to senior executives about 'letting go', forgetting about the 'hands on', and 'concentrating on the wider view' don't seem to apply to us as we start up our practices! We have to do everything and there seems so much to consider.

Chapter 12 is about marketing and, although how we obtain work is obviously of prime importance, first tackle the issues of pricing consultancy services, terms of business, contracts, business ethics, and managing travelling.

Pricing consultancy services

You will not be surprised to hear that there are no hard and fast rules on this subject!

One important point which needs to be clarified at the beginning is that 'cost' and 'price' are not the same thing. When you talk about the cost of doing something it will bear little relation to the price the client may be prepared to pay for it. It is known from studies such as PIMS (Buzzell et al, 1975) that what is most important to the client is the *perception* of 'good value for money'. If that perception can be created in the customer's mind, they will not necessarily go for the cheapest quotation. The people responsible for hiring consultants can often 'sell' the idea of using a higher-priced consultant in their organizations if it can be shown that he has the relevant experience and a good record of providing value for money. It is known that some companies will not employ 'cheaper' consultants because this would upset this 'value for money' perception. On the other hand, there are areas such as local government or the health service where it is highly likely that medium or below-medium prices will have to be charged in order to obtain the work.

There are two main points that you will have to investigate before you can decide on a pricing policy:

● You will have to work out what you need to earn, first, to cover operating expenses, and secondly, to live, that is, your annual living costs. Once you have found out what the breakeven point is, you can begin to make decisions about how many days a year you are prepared to work at what fee.

● You should find out from other consultants and from clients what the market rate is for the kind of service you offer. You will then have to decide where to place yourself on the wide range that will emerge.

As stated above, your operating expenses (that is, your non-recoverable costs) plus the amount you need to live on will give you your breakeven point. For the first year, it will be difficult to assess the expenses that may not be assigned to specific projects but they will include:

● memberships and subscriptions
● leasing office equipment
● depreciation of capital items
● running a car
● stationery
● advertising
● rent
● insurances
● taxes
● telephone

- travel
- copying and printing
- entertaining
- bank charges

You should, of course, keep strict records of all this expenditure for accounting purposes, but these records will also help you to predict the following years more accurately.

If you have the luxury of a long period of preparation before you launch out on your own, you should make a note of all these expenses to ensure that you have included all items of expenditure and to help in projecting the 'cash out' side of your cash flow.

Another important decision to make is how many days to work during the year. Although the new consultant's instinct is never to say 'no' to an offer you will not, presumably, wish to work 365 days a year! Nor, of course, will you be able to devote all your working time to consultancy. You will need time to prepare and develop work, and to spend on marketing. Your best approach may be to calculate, on the basis of your fee structure, how many days a year you need to work to break even, how many days to make a profit of x per cent and so on. You may also want to allow for holidays, voluntary work, attending conferences and other 'self-development' activities. Finally, it would be wise to include a contingency sum to accommodate days off for illness and domestic emergencies.

From asking around about market rates for consultancy, you will see that the range is enormous. Some consultants charge as little as £100 a day and the top of the international range is about £5000. You can narrow the field by asking other consultants who work in your specific area, but you will then need to match their experience and track record against yours to judge whether you can charge the same as them at the beginning. Professional institutes will also be able to give you typical ranges of fees.

In their initial fear of being short of work, there is a danger that new consultants may quote a rate which is too low to be considered a serious proposition by potential clients – all part of the 'value for money' concept. Be realistic, not too idealistic or greedy.

There are several questions you need to ask yourself when pricing your services.

Should I charge everyone the same rate?

If you are working within one specific sector, it may be possible to set a standard rate. This will be relevant to those working in specialist areas, probably with a well-defined client base.

Consultants with a broader application may consider a range of charges and this will depend on the client and the type of work to be done. For example, a consultant who runs training seminars in, say, presentation skills, may be asked to work with almost any kind of organization. In such a case, he may have a scale of charges which includes charities and voluntary organizations at the lower end and multinational companies at the upper end. The same consultant may also offer development activities which demand a greater breadth of knowledge and experience, and may involve more personal attention and follow-up than a one-off training course. This type of work would usually be charged at a higher rate.

Another method is to charge on a percentage basis. This means that the fee is based on a percentage of the total of the work involved. This has been a common practice amongst architects, for example.

Most consultants find that, even if they are tempted to work with charities and voluntary organizations for next to nothing, they should be realistic. These organizations generally expect to pay for any professional advice but may only be able to do so if the charge is less then market rates. In this way, you will also keep the relationship on a more professional level – both parties seem to feel more comfortable about their respective roles if a fee has been charged.

Should I charge a daily or hourly rate, and what are the alternatives?

First, find out what the client's expectations are in this respect. Many consultants do not do this and misunderstandings may arise if this matter is not dealt with at an early stage of the negotiations. It is common practice to quote on a daily basis although it is also usual to negotiate a fee which works out at less than a daily rate for long assignments. Some people do have an hourly rate, although this can cause administrative headaches out of proportion to the fee earned or the job satisfaction gained. A way to avoid this is to agree with the client that work can be 'saved up' until there is at least enough for half a day's fee. This is particularly relevant if travelling is involved. Another way of resolving this issue is to state that any amount of work lasting less than four hours counts as half a day for billing purposes.

Is travelling time included in the calculation of hours spent on a project?

It is usual to charge the cost of travelling while engaged on a project and this will be part of the terms of business. Whether or not it is acceptable to include travelling time as part of hours spent will depend on the nature of the project. For example, if the work entails visiting several sites during a normal working day, this time will be part of the daily calculation. If, on the other hand, you are working with a client near your base, you would be expected to put in normal working hours, and travelling to and from work would not be included in your total hours.

In all cases, ask the client, and have the agreed procedure confirmed in writing.

How do I calculate expenses?

Expenses are part of your terms of business, and this should be made clear to the client at the time of finalizing the project. (See pages 86–7.)

How do I estimate the timetable for a project?

As there are cost and price implications in estimating time to be spent on an assignment, do not commit yourself to a timetable if you are not absolutely sure of your ground. On a long project it may be helpful to work in stages, with a reassessment of timing at the end of each stage. In such a case, it is also helpful for both you and the client if you keep strict, up-to-date records of time and money spent so that an accurate budget is always available as a basis for negotiation.

Terms of business

The terms of business should be agreed with the client early on in the negotiations and clearly shown in writing, whether in a proposal, contract, letter or as a separate enclosure.

You should mention explicitly the following points.

Payment of invoices

You may prefer to have cheques paid directly into your bank account rather than sent through the post. If so, you will need to agree this with your client.

Agree a payments schedule with the client and invoice regularly. Do not save up several invoices and submit them in a block – it will wreck your cash flow and the client's confidence.

The timing of the payment of your invoices is very important because it affects your cash flow – and that is what keeps you in business. Your invoice should state when payment is due and stipulate the penalty if there is any delay. For example: 'payment is due within thirty days of the invoice date and interest will be charged at five per cent compound per month if payment is not received by the due date'.

I have recently heard several new consultants complaining that they had not yet been paid for work they had done twelve weeks previously. It transpired they did not have a written agreement with their clients – and the client had little idea of the chaos they were causing to the consultants' cash flows. Some of the larger organizations do not expect to pay within ninety days but, as most independent operators would find it difficult to maintain an acceptable cash flow in such a situation, it is best to try to negotiate a separate agreement. Indeed, many of these companies have a special arrangement for small businesses. It is, therefore, in your interest to find out what your client's procedure is in relation to payment of invoices. Some clients are even happy to agree to payment within a shorter period than one month, for example, fourteen days. Most companies appreciate that there is a difference between small businesses and the larger concerns, and will modify their rules accordingly.

Chargeable expenses

Agree in writing with the client those expenses which will be charged for separately and are not part of the fee. The type of client will often affect your attitude to expenses. Obviously, you would think twice about charging for first-class rail travel if you were working for a charity.

As shown in the sample proposal on pages 64–7, expenses will include the following items.

Travelling It is usual for consultants to charge for first-class tickets on the trains and for business-class seats on planes. Car mileage is generally charged at 30p–35p per mile (1990 prices). Taxi drivers are now used to giving receipts for business purposes. Although clients do not generally query reasonable claims without proof, they are essential for your accounts.

Hotel and subsistence If you are working away from your home base, it is normal to charge for hotel accommodation and meals not included in the hotel bill. The client company may well arrange to settle hotel bills directly if they make the booking.

Printing, copying, courier and other expenses Some consultants charge for these separately and others include them in their overall fee. If they are to be an extra charge, the client should be told at the beginning of the assignment. An alternative is to give the client any master copies of handouts and supporting material and let them arrange to do any printing or copying.

Cancellation and postponement fees

If a project, programme or course is cancelled or postponed, the results could be disastrous for your cash flow, especially if you have not agreed a scale of charges to cover this. These will vary enormously and may depend on the size of the assignment. They may be as simple as charging half the fee if the company cancels more than a month before the course and the full fee if it is cancelled with less than a month to go. A fuller version adopted by many consultants is as follows:

● more than six weeks' notice	no charge
● between four and six weeks' notice	50%
● between two and four weeks' notice	75%
● less than two weeks' notice	full charge

Expenses already incurred will be ch.. .:d in addition.

88

Development work

On a long assignment, a realistic amount of time has probably been allowed for preliminary development work. For shorter projects or for the first in a series of courses, it is usual to include in the fee a time for developing the programme and supporting materials. This may also include interviews and time for debriefing afterwards.

Contracts

In any business transaction all negotiations and agreements must be recorded in writing. Even if you are dealing with someone you know and trust, it is unwise to proceed on the basis of a 'gentleman's agreement'. You need to be covered in case of misunderstanding, foul play or misfortune, and the core document will probably be a contract, in whatever form that takes.

With some clients, particularly those in the public sector, you will have little choice about signing a contract, as they provide a proforma which includes specific clauses about methods of payment, expenses and so on. Usually, there is not much room for negotiation in these cases but, if you are unhappy with any of the content, check with your legal adviser and make your feelings known to the client.

Where no such formal contract exists, agree with the client the procedure you will follow. It may be as simple as writing a letter which confirms the consultant's appointment to carry out a specific task. As shown on pages 64–7, the proposal may also double as a contract if the client gives written confirmation that it is acceptable to her.

Other contracts

You may also need to draw up agreements with sub-contractors and anyone else who works with you. These will state cancellation/postponement agreements between you and them as well as a schedule of their payments.

Contracts with sub-contractors will be similar to those you enter into with a client. You will agree to pay an agreed amount for specific work and you will explain which expenses are acceptable, when invoices should be submitted, and so on. In some cases, you may wish to include a clause which prevents the sub-contractor taking advantage of the contact with your client to sell her own services. You should discuss this with your legal adviser as the law in this area is tricky.

If you employ any staff on a permanent basis, you will have to draw up a contract of employment and, again, your legal adviser will be able to help you with this.

Ethics

The subject of business ethics is becoming increasingly debated in the United Kingdom. There is an argument that it has always been an important part of business but there is also a point of view that thinking in this area until now has been woolly and ill-defined. The first issue is that of the ethical relationship between you and your client. Secondly, with the growing awareness of environmental issues and ethical investments, people are also asking questions about whether organizations should operate in parts of the world that are considered unacceptable in terms of human rights or about the type of industry an organization is part of, for example, armaments or tobacco.

Typical comments from consultants on these issues are as follows:

- 'I wouldn't work for any organization with a South African connection.'
- 'I would not work for a second time with people who did not treat their people well or for those whose company culture I didn't feel sympathy for.'

A not-so-typical reaction was:

- 'I might even consider South Africa because you can learn from these situations.'

Consultants may have to confront ethical issues frequently during their work. They need to make conscious decisions about which type of organizations or industries they will not work for and, if they have not approved of the way a client operates during a project, they may well decide not to work for them again, even if a lucrative contract were offered.

Many professions have Codes of Professional Conduct which go some way towards defining an ethical approach for their members.

Any consultant will, however, also need to draw up a personal code and this may need to be modified as new situations arise and have to be dealt with.

Amongst the responsibilities a consultant has towards his clients is confidentiality. Clients rightly expect that you will not discuss their projects with other people, whether competitors or not, or gossip about the company and its employees, test scores, financial position and so on.

Another aspect of confidentiality is the use of clients' names for marketing purposes. Some clients do not like it generally known that they are using consultants, especially if that consultant is generally recognized as specialist in, for example, resolving problems among Boards of Directors. The simple way round this is to ask clients if you may add their name to your list of organizations who use you, and to respect their answer – whatever it is.

When you have completed successful assignment, news will spread that you have done a good job, and companies from the same industry may ask you to consider working with them as well. Check back with the original client to see that they have no objection to your working in these other organizations. If your original client believes that you will respect the confidentiality of any information you have gained during the project, they do not usually put any barriers in your way.

Other ethical issues that may arise include the situation where a client suggests to you that, whatever conclusions you reach during the assignment, you are expected to write a report that confirms what she wants to recommend. It may also be suggested that you omit certain information from your report or that you minimize certain, possibly critical, aspects of your investigation. You will have to make up your own mind in such situations. Some consultants would say that, as the client has hired you and is paying you, you should concur with her request. Ultimately, your own conscience must guide you on these issues.

In his book *How to Succeed as an Independent Consultant*, Herman Holtz (1988) suggests:

I recommend the following code of ethics for your serious consideration:

- Make no extravagant promises, verbal or written, that you would be unwilling or unable to live up to.
- Do not withhold important facts or hype the truth to deliberately

mislead the client, inducing him or her to believe something you did not explicitly say.
- Be scrupulous in respecting the confidentiality of every client's proprietory information and what your business relationships with clients have been.
- Make a strictly honest accounting of hours, when the contract calls for it, and be up front with all clients and prospective clients.
- Refrain from denouncing or condemning competitors.
- Make it a policy to deliver everything you promise a client.
- Conduct yourself with professional dignity in all matters and at all times.

Relationship with the client

This aspect is very much tied in with your approach to ethical issues as well as reflecting your level of personal and communication skills. Relationships, both personal and contractual, have to be handled professionally and with integrity.

When you agree to take on a project, make sure you know who you are reporting to and who is responsible for the assignment. You must know who you should go to for clarification, arbitration, agreement or confirmation on any issue. Be aware of the 'coalition of clients' (see Chapter 12).

As a consultant with knowledge about a company's current situation and future plans, you may be tempted to speculate on the financial markets. Beware – consultants to companies in the United Kingdom can be sued under insider trading laws. It is best to declare any shareholding you have in a client company before you start, and to take legal advice should you wish to buy or sell shares during or after your time with the company.

If you are successful in one project and move through the company, make sure the original client does not 'lose face'. Keep the original client informed as much as possible – though this may not be easy if the new contact does not want the original one to be involved.

Travelling and scheduling

Dealing with the stress of frequent travelling is covered in Chapter 9. But there is another aspect of travelling, and that is how it affects the way you conduct your practice. If you are working on your own with no support or the minimum of back-up help, you may well worry about what happens to clients, existing and potential, if you are away from base for more than a few days. Much of this will be made easier by the use of modern telecommunications and will be discussed further in the following section on the office. Careful scheduling should also enable you to give adequate time to each client and project to make them feel that you are looking after them well.

If you try and cram too much into a day, clients will soon begin to feel neglected and you will be increasingly less effective as you become more and more exhausted and panicky. Not only is it advisable not to fill the diary to capacity each day but you should also have the confidence to say 'no' to clients if they demand meetings or papers at unrealistically short notice. Many consultants have found that, if they explain to clients that they are unable to attend a meeting tomorrow but could manage the next day, this is generally acceptable. If you keep clients well informed about your movements, especially if you are travelling abroad, they will usually be flexible in their demands upon your time, as long as the project is completed by the agreed date and to their satisfaction.

If you travel a great deal – and particularly if you spend long periods overseas – make sure your clients are aware of it. As long as they know when you are going away and how they can send messages to you if necessary, they will not worry unduly.

If you are clear about the principles which determine the way you run your practice and behave towards your clients, you will feel confident that you are offering a competitive, value-for-money service to clients who know they can trust you and enjoy working with you, as well as being respected by your fellow consultants for your professional approach.

11 The Infrastructure

The support structure you build for yourself should be designed to allow you to spend most of your time doing what you want to do, that is, working as an independent consultant. The bulk of this infrastructure will be based in the office and it is worth devoting some time to this to make sure you do a good job – it can be very expensive if you get it wrong!

The office

As well as operating as a consultant, you will also become an expert on all aspects of running an office – the best word processors, the easiest filing system, the most comfortable chairs, the similarity between photocopiers, the staggering range of typewriter ribbons and the seduction of beautiful stationery. Most people who start up on their own will have little experience of what actually makes an office work and they may well be confused by what is available in the shops. If you are not sure what is needed and what is value for money in this area, ask someone who has the necessary knowledge to come and help you. If you know a well-trained and experienced secretary, she may be willing to help you go through brochures or look round office supplies shops.

A typical shopping list will contain the following items.

94

Business stationery

You will need to have a minimum of letterheads, business cards and compliment slips printed at the beginning. Other items may be folders, fax and telex forms, report covers, message pads, memo forms, invoices and proformas for proposals/contracts. You may not need all of these, so it is worth waiting a few months to see how often you use them before you incur expenditure on designers and printing.

Unless you are a competent designer and setter of Letraset, it is worth employing someone to design your stationery and logo. The logo does not have to be elaborate and may simply consist of your name or the name you have chosen for your practice in an attractive typeface.

The minimum information you will need on a letterhead is as follows:

- name
- address
- telephone number (with international code if you have overseas contacts)
- fax number
- telex number   } if appropriate
- VAT number

Depending on your situation you may also need to include:

- address of registered office
- names of directors

It will be useful to ask an experienced typist to check that the letterhead works – often something that looks wonderful is difficult to work with in practice. For example, lining the main body of the letter up with the printed heading may make the letter look lopsided or there may not be enough room to type in a long address.

As there are now excellent print shops in most cities and towns, you will be able to organize repeat orders of your stationery once you have the original artwork. You do not need to consult a designer each time you need fresh stocks of paper, provided you ensure that they give you the artwork for which you have paid.

Office equipment and furniture

The design of the basic office desk and chair has changed out of all recognition over the past few years. In particular, much more attention is being paid to the design of chairs so that they do not damage your back and other parts of your body. A well-designed chair is expensive, but is worth the investment and, even if you make do with a trestle table to work on at first, please do not spare the expenditure on a good chair. (See also Chapter 13.)

Your workplace is a very important part of how you operate. You have to feel comfortable there and it is worth spending some time designing it to suit you. If you are left-handed, for example, some of the standard units may not fit in with the way you work – shelves or drawers may be on the wrong side for you and will add to the stress you place on your body when sitting at the desk.

Many pieces of office equipment may be leased and this has several advantages: payments may be monthly or quarterly instead of a lump sum; they are claimable against tax; and the equipment can be easily up-graded. The following items of equipment fall into this category.

Telephone There is a bewildering choice of systems, handsets and options now available. If you are working from home, you may use the same phone number but you may also consider installing a system that allows you to have a separate business line and fax line. This is a little more expensive, but it should give you priority with the telephone company if anything goes wrong. It also has the added advantage of allowing the home and office to operate independently of each other.

You may wish to use a telephone answering service if you prefer that to an answering machine. Ask other consultants to recommend a good service, or ask the telephone suppliers, or look in your commercial directories, such as Yellow Pages in the United Kingdom.

Fax You can have a fax incorporated into your telephone system as an alternative to having a separate machine. With some machines you have to use a switch system where a recorded message asks you either to send the fax or to wait until the phone is answered in the normal way. It is worth considering whether this conveys the appropriate professional image. Also, some callers from abroad may not understand what is going on!

The use of fax has increased enormously over the last few years and has replaced telex in many instances. If you have clients or other contacts abroad, a fax is an invaluable means of communication, particularly when different time zones make it inconvenient to talk on the phone with, for example, clients in Australia or the United States. It also keeps costs down as it reduces the temptation for small talk. Clients are increasingly expecting that you will have a fax. But if you cannot justify the cost of a fax machine initially, there are now good fax bureaux starting up in most towns and cities.

Telex   Dealing with some countries means that telex is still the most effective means of communication, although even places with the most suspect telecommunication systems are beginning to use fax more and more. Telex has become increasingly sophisticated, with the use of software packages in personal computers to replace many of the cumbersome machines that used to be commonplace. Again, there are now bureaux and agencies which will send and receive telexes for you if it is not economically viable for you to have your own system.

Typewriter/word processor/desktop publishing   You will need to be realistic about what you need. Some of the typewriters on the market are very advanced and, with storage facilities, limited display, choice of typefaces and many other features, may be adequate for your practice. Some may be able to double up as letter quality printers for computers if appropriate.

Word processing software is becoming more user friendly and if you cannot use a keyboard there are now packages which will teach you directly from the screen.

If you have to produce large quantities of printed material, handouts, brochures and so on, you may consider it worthwhile investing in a desktop publishing system. These are very expensive but do produce a wide range of documents, with the possibility of pictures and other visual aids.

Speak to other consultants about their experiences using computers. Be very clear about what it is that you need from your system and persuade the suppliers that their systems must fit your needs and not the other way round.

Answering machine   There are those who believe that clients will be hostile towards a consultant who uses an answering machine rather than an answering service. I am not convinced that this is true, but it is worth shopping round to find the machine that suits you best and leaves the best impression with callers. Potential clients are more likely to leave a message or call back if their calls are dealt with by an answering machine rather than an unanswered ringing.

If you are away from base frequently, you will need a system that will enable you to take messages off your machine from wherever you are, to change the message by remote control, and/or page you.

Photocopier   Be realistic about your needs. The capacity, size, cost and robustness of copiers varies enormously. If you have only a few copies to make from time to time, you may be able to manage using a local print shop or, if you are lucky, a fellow consultant who works nearby. Most fax machines also have the capability of copying single sheets and this may be worth considering if your volume is low. The size of your copier may be determined by the space you have available. Our choice depended entirely on whether it could get up the spiral stairs into the office!

Dictating machine/tape recorder   These machines may be used for recording meetings (with the agreement of others present), for dictating letters and reports to be typed later or for making notes during site visits, train journeys or car journeys. Remember that it is illegal to use them while driving unless they are voice-activated.

Portable telephone/car phone   Sometimes a mixed blessing! If you have a portable phone, you may need to be discreet in its use, especially when dealing with clients' confidential information. If you really need a car phone (and think of the peace without one!), the same rule applies as for dictating in the car.

Car

The most explosive, emotional and politically fought issue I come across with all levels of manager is the company car policy – who is given which type and with what extras!

For consultants the choice of car depends on two often incompatible dimensions – practicability and status. Practicability should come first. A simple listing of the performance specifications for your work will help:

● Will I be doing mostly local runs or hundreds of miles per day on motorways?

- Will it be mainly one or two people using the car, or the family and others?
- Will there be a lot of stop–start driving or lots of smooth running?
- Will I need to carry a lot of kit for my consultancy?
- Will I need space so that I can use the car as an office as well?
- What will the capital and running costs need to be?

I have seen a vast range of consultants' cars in my time from clapped-out Marina Estates covered in dog hairs and baby seats, to BMWs which the young consultants seem to consider *de rigueur*, to Porsches into which it is impossible to put a flipchart stand, and even to a white Rolls Royce complete with mobile phone, fax and a well-stocked drinks cabinet!

Cost, both capital and running, will play a key part. Do you need to buy a new car? Depreciation on buying a brand new car is horrific in the first few months, so why not buy a slightly used car and at least save some of your cash flow? What about getting an up-market 'warranted' car which may be a year or two old but is guaranteed well maintained?

Should you lease or buy? Your tax adviser needs to be consulted to see what is best for your tax position and your tax flow. In theory, leasing will help your cash flow but could adversely affect your tax position. What is best for you?

As for status and your car – I enter this field on tiptoe. The advertisers have worked so well on this that it is easy to describe people simply as a brand and type of car. If it is important to you that you live up to the advertisers' image, then I hope you can generate the cash to do so. One point I will make is to ask you to be careful in relation to the type of cars your clients have. I have a client whose 'policy' on cars is to buy British for managers at all levels. At the top they could have Granada Scorpios but not Jaguars. An enormous amount of time was spent studying the new Scorpio list each year to see what extras could be bolted on. The situation was not improved when a computer consultant started turning up in a Jaguar XJ-S Cabriolet, sending the client's directors into paroxysms of envy. He did not realise this, of course, and kept boasting about his 'nice little motor'. Once he had completed his project, he was not invited back. My advice, therefore, is either to conform to your clients' norm, or compete but on another dimension – which could mean having some outrageous Japanese or Italian beast, or a vintage or classic car – one that says 'I'm meant to be different from you, rather than better than you'.

Our own eccentricity is not to have a car at all. Living in central London with easy access to transport of all kinds (including exotic car hire companies), and travelling large distances most days, I rely on trains and planes to do my driving, then use a taxi at the other end. This has opened my eyes to another underused perk of senior managers – the company chauffeur. For consultants, they are superb sources of company micropolitical information and can help interpret what is really going on in your work. They tell me that they are usually underemployed, but both they and their bosses are delighted to be able to show that there are other uses for them than just ferrying the boss to and from work. I have been taken on some extraordinarily long and helpful journeys across country to get a 'better' train or plane by these folk – for which many thanks.

If you are really going to compete in the 'status stakes' in a serious way, then you can claim success when you arrive – as I saw an international business consultant do recently – in a Bentley Camargue with your own chauffeur!

The health aspects of driving a car are covered in Chapter 13.

Filing

Keep filing as simple as possible. Again, if you are not quite sure of the best way to tackle the subject, ask someone who knows. There are many systems on the market, many different types of cupboards, cabinets and trolleys with files and folders in a variety of colours and sizes. You may well settle for a combination of cupboards or cabinets for archive material and less-used papers, with a trolley for current projects and information. Trolleys have the advantage of accessibility and they can also tuck away under a worktop or desk when not in use.

The actual filing system you use will depend on the type of work you do but always keep it simple. You may be the only person who uses it now, but if you take on extra help or work with another consultant they will also need to understand it.

The other piece of advice about filing is – do it every day. If you do not, it piles up, becomes crumpled and mislaid, and you waste valuable time looking for it. Five minutes every day saves a great deal of frustration later on.

Keeping records

Records can now be kept mostly on the computer but may also be done manually without spending too much in maintaining the systems once they are established. Your accountant will advise you as to what records you should keep and you should find all the necessary books in a good stationery shop.

Records under the following headings are important.

Accounts On the income side, you are legally obliged to keep copies of your invoices for your own records as well as for your accountant, as they will show earnings and VAT. With regard to expenditure, you are legally obliged to keep all your receipts, cheque stubs, bank statements, petty cash vouchers, bills from suppliers and any other record of money spent. Design a way of recording all outgoing post, especially if you are able to claim back for postage. It is also useful to have a record of when you send out post in case there is ever a query.

Profit and loss accounts, balance sheets, cash flows and time and money budgets have all been mentioned previously, and form part of the management accounts that you need to ensure you always have access to information which tells you how the business is performing.

Client and project records Always keep accurate and full records of all contacts with a client, existing or potential. One new consultant recently told me that the one thing she had learned to her cost since becoming independent was the need to have all conversations and negotiations written down and kept on file. It also makes your life easier if you open a file immediately you make contact with a client so that you can always lay your hands on basic information such as contact names, phone numbers, when you first spoke, who was involved and so on.

Keep formal records or timesheets of how much time you spend on each project. This will not only help you to draw up invoices but will also enable you to make accurate forecasts for future assignments. Included under this heading may be a timetable for the project, showing the different activities involved and when they should be completed. The simplest way to do this is to divide tasks into those which have to be done at a specific time – and mark them into their place on the timetable – and those which are more flexible, that is, which can be fitted in to the blank spaces.

Some consultants find it useful to draw up a 'post mortem' sheet after each assignment. This is a brief summary of what went well, what could be done better next time, the names of people and companies that were helpful or those who should be ignored another time, and any surprises that turned up so that you can be ready for similar occurrences on future assignments.

Practice records   These will include such things as details of lease agreements, maintenance agreements on equipment, and stock records (so that you do not run the risk of running out of essential stationery accessories at a crucial time). Some of these will need to be cross-referenced to items in the financial records.

If you work with other consultants at any stage, you should keep details of them in case you require to contact them again. Details of time they have spent on projects will be cross-referenced from the assignment records. Also, a reliable card index system of addresses and phone numbers is an invaluable asset and should be kept scrupulously up to date. Over the years, this becomes an almost priceless point of reference.

If you use credit cards for both personal and professional reasons, it will be worthwhile registering those cards under a protection scheme. These are operated through the banks and credit card companies. It is also useful to have a record of card numbers in case of abuse by others, theft and loss.

Personal   All insurance and other policies should be kept safely, but readily accessible for regular updating.

If you attend conferences, training courses or seminars, make a note of them for inclusion in your CV if appropriate. Also, if you give lectures or talks in a personal capacity, contacts may follow and it is useful to have a record of the occasion and what you said.

'Self-development' is looked at further in Chapter 13 and you should keep a record of what activities you take part in while broadening your skills and knowledge. Check them against the checklists in Chapter 2.

Wills might seem a grisly subject, but it is essential to have one because if you do not, and die intestate, you will condemn your family to years of uncertainty and possible penury.

Diaries and other planning aids

Diaries are not generally used in a very worthwhile way. They can be invaluable planning tools and also act as a repository of all sorts of useful information, reminding you of meetings, anniversaries, money spent, people spoken to, mislaid phone numbers, social occasions and reports to be prepared.

Many consultants design their own diary sheets or use one of the many systems now on the market. Even the simplest desk diary can be modified to be used in a way that does away with most of the extra pieces of paper with scribbled notes that most of us resort to. If you draw a wide margin on the right hand side of each page and mark that column 'To Do', you have straightaway given yourself space to write down tasks that need to be done. You can then allocate priorities to each task and give yourself the satisfaction of ticking them off as each one is completed. You can also include lists of people to write to or phone, reminders of birthdays and social occasions, tickets to buy and bills to pay.

In the stationery shops, you will find a huge variety of wall planners, charts and other methods of helping you organize your life in the most effective way. Look for the way that suits you best. All of the systems available have their merits but they may not fit in with what you need and, as with the computer software, you want it to match your particular requirements. You should not have to make do with a system that does not fully meet those requirements.

Administrative help

At the beginning you may have to do all your own typing, filing, phone calls, photocopying and ordering office supplies. If you have no previous experience of administration work, you may find it tedious and time-consuming and will be tempted to delay it. In such a situation, you will probably employ someone to help out at the earliest possible opportunity.

If you do not have keyboard skills, acquire them as quickly as possible and you will never again have to rely on anyone else for the production of material. With the new technology, you are in a position to change and move text around relatively easily, and much time can be saved when compared with dictating or writing out a first draft and then altering that.

The other routine administrative duties are the ones which you may wish to delegate to someone else, as you neither gain any satisfaction nor increase your knowledge by continuing to do them. You may not require someone to help on a regular basis, just occasionally for a few hours. There are freelance secretaries who are prepared to work in this way and you can find out who they are by asking around or perhaps advertising locally.

There are also bureaux which offer secretarial, typing and word processing services on an hourly basis. If your base is away from a centre which is large enough to have such a bureau, you may have more difficulty in finding someone to help you. Non-urgent work may be dictated onto tape and sent to a bureau or freelance secretary by post or courier and returned in the same way.

If you do take on someone to help, you may have to learn some new skills or modify some old ones. Very few people are taught how to dictate, to a person or into a machine, and now might be the time to learn or perfect the technique. The best person to ask is the person who will be taking the dictation or transcribing the tape. Find out from her what the best practice is, and you will soon improve.

If you submit manuscripts for typing, look at the quality of the material you are handing over. Be honest with yourself about its legibility and the clarity of your instructions and, again, ask the typist for her opinion. It is only good manners to present work that is of an acceptable standard. The reverse side of this coin is, of course, that you will receive work back much more quickly and with more chance of it being accurate.

Good secretarial and clerical help can make all the difference to the way you feel about the office and your work. It is in your interests to build up a sound relationship with this person, so that she becomes a reliable support to your efforts and a valuable team member.

When you take on administrative help, you need to choose someone who has certain basic skills and qualities. The following checklist may be a useful start.

SKILLS	QUALITIES
Technical:	Unflappable
• WP/computer	Sense of humour
• Typing	Reliable
• Shorthand	Loyal
• Audio	Trustworthy

104

- Fax
- Bookkeeping/Accounts
- Deciphering writing

Communication:
- Written
- Spoken
- Interpersonal
- Assertive
- Telephone
- Listening
- Proofreading

Organizational:
- Systems
- Priorities
- Memory
- Routines
- 'Juggling'

Common sense
Flexible
Punctual
Tidy
Adaptable
Initiative

It is tempting to surround yourself with all the trappings of a successful business. Make sure that you have everything that you need to do your work in the most efficient way possible but do not waste valuable resources on 'just-in-case' or 'I've-always-wanted-one-of-those' articles. Shop around and ask other people's advice before you commit yourself to large expenditure. After operating for a few months, you will begin to realize what you need to help you become effective as a consultant, and, if you have the opportunity to seek the advice of someone who seems to you to be an organized and effective administrator, so much the better.

12 Marketing your Services

I have divided this chapter into three sections, as follows:

1   the first looks at potential clients and where they may be found;
2   the second considers how you will publicize your services; and
3   the third asks how you will sell your services.

To begin with I think it would be helpful to clarify the difference between 'marketing' and 'selling'. Selling is only a part of the marketing process and it cannot take place successfully until a marketing review and sales plan has been drawn up. You therefore need to carry out the following tasks:

- Analyse the changing market – forecast who is likely to need your services and why – and learn to understand and be sensitive to your market by constantly reviewing the trends. A method of doing this is illustrated in Chapter 14.
- Assess your own strengths and weaknesses, and also where your interests lie. The lists are not always similar.
- Consider where you want to put your limited resources during the next six months, one year, two years.
- Draw up your plan for the future.

This marketing plan will identify, categorize, target and contact potential clients. You will then need to examine how you will make yourself known to these 'prospects'.

The selling part of the process comes when prospective clients have agreed to talk to you about what you have to offer and you then have to convince them that your service or product is the most suitable for their needs. A frontal assault using 'cold call' telephoning or letter writing is rarely helpful until you are sure what it is you are offering, to whom, why and at what price.

Many books and authorities on consulting and setting up small businesses devote a large part of their discussion to marketing. It is a crucially important part of being in business, and you should always be aware of and sensitized to opportunities when they arise, as these will be part of your future stream of income. Many consultants do not enjoy the marketing side of their work. They would rather be working with the established client but, often grudgingly, accept that they need to keep their names and skills in front of prospective clients if they are to maintain a regular and interesting scope of projects. Repeat business is certainly evidence of success, but a consultancy based on only a very few clients and mostly repeat business is strategically weak, and may face hard times if an established client is unable to continue for any reason, particularly if their external environment is changing – due to merger or takeover at the level of the client company, or through structural change in the industry, or because of growing competition.

When scheduling your time for the next few months, include space for marketing, formal or informal, direct or indirect. However busy you are now, you may well have nothing to fall back on when this rush is over. That is when the cash flow problems begin. At the beginning of your practice, you may spend a higher percentage of your time on marketing than when you are well established, and this should be done in a thorough and logical way.

A recent survey of consultants (GMS Consultancy, 1990), shows that 'the most prosperous freelances did not think of downtime as a bugbear. They saw it as a space for extra marketing and other development work.'

If you are clear in your mind about what clients are looking for in the consultants they employ, you will find it easier to convey that image in your marketing strategy. The skills and qualities listed in Chapter 2 could form a starting point for such a strategy.

Where and who are your potential clients?

Consultants must be aware of the likely main sources of potential clients, as well as of other prospects. The location and nature of these clients may also have a bearing on how consultants set up and conduct their operations.

You may be in the fortunate position of starting your practice with a full workload. This means that you will already have a good idea of the kind of organization that is likely to use you. If you are working with a large or medium-sized organization and you are judged to be successful, you may well receive repeat work. In the larger organizations which are made up of several smaller companies or autonomous divisions, you may find yourself moving round as you acquire a broad overview of the whole place.

If you are starting from scratch, you should be aware of all the options.

1　Large organizations do use large consultancies and it is often difficult for independent practitioners to obtain work from these companies. However, there are some well-known and long-established consultants who have made their mark on such organizations as 'niche' players. They do not purport to be able to do large-scale, number-crunching type work but offer a personalized, high value-added service to, usually, senior executives. Often these relationships are long term, and the consultant is rated by the client as highly cost-effective as a sounding board and source of alternative views.

2　Medium-sized companies may not be able to afford certain specialists on a permanent basis; so, because they are constantly changing and/or growing, they may need occasional service from outsiders for specific help for specific periods or projects. Their cost-effectiveness here is to help the company deliver a specific assignment (often a change project) on time, to quality and to cost.

3　Small businesses may be a fruitful source of income, especially if you have specialist knowledge in this area. A large number of small businesses fail each year because they do not have experience of handling the problems that result from growth. Cost-effectiveness here can be in helping both the growth of the business *and* the growth of the people involved.

4　Some individuals may need the help of a consultant, particularly in the financial field (tax, investment) property, design (interior, graphic, fashion) or personal health and growth.

5 The large consultancies may be a source of work. When they win large contracts, they are sometimes short of particular skills and will have to sub-contract, often at good rates. However, one disadvantage may be that you will have to represent their 'party line', which may not always be yours.

6 As the public sector is increasingly moving towards a 'market basis', many new opportunities with local and central government departments and agencies are occurring. These organizations are often unused to working with consultants and tend to have a stereotype thought that all consultancies are like the large international firms that most people have heard of. They are not good either at paying market rates, or paying on time. You need to be tough on the contractual terms of business so they do not bankrupt you unwittingly by not paying your bill for three or four months. The potential for good work in this area is high – but so are the risks, as the clients tend to be unskilled in working with consultants. You will need to become familiar with procedures, contacts and how the bureaucracies work.

7 International agencies such as the World Bank, EC, International Labour Office, other United Nations agencies, and national development agencies may be attractive to those who wish to work overseas, particularly in developing countries. These organizations are used to working with consultants. The rates are low to middling, but the prestige and contacts make them attractive to many.

Keep up to date with local, national and international events, especially those that may lead to consultancy opportunities. Become an avid absorber of information, read a wide range of newspapers, journals and magazines, and the lists of recent appointments in organizations, and be aware of the financial situation of companies in the sector in which you wish to work.

Create files of areas of present interest and present clients, so that you are always up to date on the media's comments on them. Even more important, create files on potential clients, developing issues, industries, services, regions or countries which interest you. Constant scanning of the environment allows you to intervene at the right time, rather than blundering in with a good idea at the wrong time, thereby souring your chances.

Volume, price and cost

As Mr Micawber states, in *David Copperfield*: 'Annual income twenty pounds, annual expenditure nineteen pounds six, result happiness. Annual income twenty pounds, annual expenditure twenty pounds, ought and six, result misery.' As you are running yourself as a business, it is necessary to use the same basic principles as any commercial organization. Mr Micawber is a useful hero to keep in mind – provided you stay on the 'happiness' side of his equation, that is, always try to have an annual surplus rather than deficit and keep a positive cash flow.

The three main variables when you have the business running are:

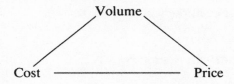

You have the ability to adjust any or all of these. For example, if you operate in a sector where your service has many competitors, then it is in the dangerous area of being 'commoditized' in the client's mind. This means that there will be little to differentiate the competitors except price, so that is what you have to compete on. This is true from supermarkets to financial services, and it is a dangerous position to be in unless you can either improve volume (improve work volume/throughput) for the same input and/or cut your costs. However, cutting costs in a service industry needs to be done carefully or the clients will complain of a drop in the quality of service.

Think of the flexibility you have with pricing. Most consultants are binary on this point. They are either terrified at suggesting a price rise or are unrealistically euphoric at 'cracking the £1000 a day barrier' immediately. First, you need to find out the range of prices others charge for your sort of service. Then you need to check that the quality you give is *perceived* by your clients as in the upper quartile of the consultants they have used. You do this by asking them to rank you alongside others they have used. Perception is everything here. Clients will pay a premium price for perceived quality and consistency – and can sell this on, if necessary, in their organizations.

Calculating volume, price and cost is therefore essential in a marketing review leading to a sales plan. The big question is, 'What is each client buying by using me?' The answers are often surprising. They could be: certainty of delivery; prestige; acknowledged quality; cheapness; and so on. One of my husband's clients, the managing director of one of the United Kingdom's biggest companies, is explicit: 'I use you because of your incredible breadth of experience across industries and nations. It's really refreshing to hear how others have had completely different thoughts on age-old organizational problems – it gives perspective to what we're doing and lets us take wise decisions within our culture. If I didn't do my job, which I love, the only other one in the world I'd like is yours!'

How will you publicize your services?

Different types of consultancy require different methods of publicity. Some of these techniques are shown below.

Advertising

Brochure An informative, stylishly designed brochure is useful, particularly if your field of operation is well defined. For those consultants who wear several different hats, it may be more appropriate to produce several loose-leaf sheets, each describing a specific activity, rather than a folded brochure. In this way, only the pages relevant to a client's needs will be used. A brochure should be attractive visually, giving adequate but not too much information, clearly written and concise. Information should not get out of date too quickly and key points should be clearly indicated.

Direct mail You may have an extensive list of prospective or existing clients and you will build on this over the years. You can also buy or rent mailing lists through brokers or specialist advertising agencies. Some professional bodies also have their own directories of members which would give you access to specific groups of people.

Sending a personalized letter, produced on a word processor, with a copy of your brochure, is probably the most effective use of a mailing list. You will appreciate that your material has to stand out from a mountain of paper received in organizations every day. The response rate is low and it may be several weeks or months before you receive any reaction. You need, therefore, to bear in mind such factors as the current economic climate, the cyclical nature (if any) of the area you work in and so on.

You must follow up these letters after a few days, not only because it shows prospects that you are serious but also because you will be able to build up a database about which lists are the most effective.

Advertisements   Most consultants do not consider this a professional approach to publicizing their services. There may, however, be occasions when it might produce results. For example, if you are experienced in small business management, a well-placed advertisement in a specialist journal or the literature for a specialist conference may catch the eye of someone needing that particular help.

Registers   Many professional bodies keep a list of people who are willing for their names to be put forward for work on projects in specific areas. You may wish to place your name on such a register.

Announcements   If you are running a public seminar, giving a lecture or organizing a conference, you may wish to advertise this by putting an announcement in a newspaper or journal.

Word of mouth   The best advertisement for you is a satisfied client who praises you to another potential client. Although this method is necessarily slow, it is remarkably effective. It can be helped if you write up your work and the issues stemming from it, with the client's agreement (they will often insist it is anonymous), in the professional journals or even the mass media.

Networking

For many consultants, networking is one of the most enjoyable aspects of working independently. It is the building and developing of contacts at many levels – professional, client, social, business associates, other consultants. It is a comparatively cost-effective way of keeping your face and name in people's minds and there are several ways of doing it.

Membership You will gain more from joining a few carefully chosen associations than becoming a member of many. Your aim should be not only to develop links with as many potential clients as possible, but also to keep up to date with best practice in your own specialist field as part of your continuing education and development. The range is wide and will include professional, business or trade association as well as organizations such as Chambers of Commerce, Rotarians, Soroptimists, various women's groups and many others. Choose associations where you can play a medium- to high-profile role, so that you become known.

Speaking, lecturing, teaching In addition to being a member of a few associations, you may consider offering your services as a speaker at meetings, teaching at colleges, polytechnics or universities, or giving lectures for your professional body. Not everybody enjoys this kind of public speaking but it is an excellent way of making contacts and it is a skill which may be learned.

Seminars, workshops and conferences Events of this kind have a two-way benefit. If you attend as a participant, you will make new contacts and consolidate old ones, as well as developing your skills and knowledge. If you are on the organizing committee or speaking yourself, you can take advantage of the excellent opportunity to make yourself known to a wider group of people.

The media

Discretion is needed here. Bob Garratt had a client who was keen to be written up in a national daily newspaper, using the company's name. The article was about director development and sounded very exciting. Unfortunately, when the article was published, the company's share price fell, because the brokers decided that, if its directors needed development, then it could not be properly run! As the company was one of less than 10 per cent of UK companies who actually do anything about director development, this adverse publicity seemed somewhat unfair, but it proved a salutary lesson for all.

Talking on local, regional or national radio or TV on topical issues does help, however. Many items are re-broadcast on the BBC World Service and you may receive responses from the most unlikely places.

Writing Publishing books and articles may not make you much money, but they will make sure your name becomes familiar to many people. Consultants who have written books have generally been pleased with the number of contacts they have made as a result of their publication. Articles in appropriate newspapers, journals, magazines and newsletters are also useful in developing your own ideas as well as publicizing your services, and they can form the basis of a letter to existing clients enclosing your latest piece. This keeps your name in front of them.

Radio and TV If you have been involved in any research, have written on a topical subject, have been involved in a particularly interesting project or have spoken recently to a prestigious gathering, you may well be invited to appear on radio or TV. Consultants are increasingly being asked to participate in news or discussion programmes. You might also consider sending a news release to the media if you are publishing a book or the results of research.

Public relations (PR)

Some consultants hire a PR consultant to promote their services. They take on the routine work of contacting the media. You still have to provide the copy, but they can focus it for you. Expect to pay £200–£1000 per day for their services. This may be too expensive for many people when just starting up, but it may be worth considering later on.

How will you sell your services?

Selling your services comes quite a long way down the marketing process. When you have defined your skills, identified prospects, publicized your services and followed up any leads, you will then meet potential clients. This is when you start selling face to face. The first opportunity for a face-to-face discussion with a prospective client sets the tone for your future relationship. The meeting may be a formal occasion, with several representatives from the organization, or informal, perhaps a lunch for just two of you.

While you may appear relaxed and confident to the client, you will only feel that way if you keep several points in mind.

1 Preparing thoroughly for the meeting is crucial. Find out as much as you can about the organization and, if possible, the person you are going to see. Use the electronic databases available in libraries to find out the latest media information on them. Then, by asking a few relevant questions at the beginning of the interview to check out your background research, you will also show that you have prepared yourself well.

2 You will already have sent a CV. At the meeting, however, you should say a little about yourself so that personal contacts may be made, but do not spend most of the time talking about yourself and boosting your own image.

Encourage the client to tell you about the organization, and the general problems facing them. By careful questioning, narrow those problems down to the 'real' issues. When you have identified the needs, repeat them back to the client and record them. You will have to assure the client, tactfully, that they are not peculiar to his organization – unless they are! There are rarely new needs, just more effective ways of dealing with existing problems in their particular cultural context.

Do not try to guess what clients want. If you ask discriminating questions, they will tell you what the problems are and may also hint at the type of solution they would find acceptable. Use *their* words to repeat back what you are hearing, even when you can sense that there are words behind the words. Show you are listening attentively.

3 As you explain what you have to offer, you must be wary of giving away too much 'free' consulting. It is usual not to charge for this first exploratory meeting, but it is unwise to give the prospective client all the clues to the solution of his problems at that meeting. Be honest if you cannot help – it builds your credibility, particularly if you can direct them to someone else who can.

4 All meetings should end with everyone knowing what the next step will be. If the signs have been positive, you will agree to a specific action, for example, submitting a proposal and price, or giving a presentation to a specified client group.

You will not often sign a contract at a first meeting. Other people from the client organization may need to be involved, or some negotiation may have to take place on issues such as fees, timing or programme. But stay in close touch with your contacts, moving them firmly towards a decision.

5 Make notes during your meeting if at all possible. Most clients will prefer this to the use of a tape recorder, particularly at this early stage. It is hard to remember everything that happens during a discussion, so the art of accurate note-taking, especially when closely involved in the discussion at the same time, is worth developing.

6 Learn to distinguish between prospective clients who are seriously considering employing you and those who are perhaps just seeking some free advice. To help you make this decision, try to establish some key points:

● Who is the real decision-maker? Does the person you are talking to have the authority to agree your appointment or is he acting as a filter for someone else? If the latter, try to speak to the actual decision-maker as soon a possible. There is rarely one single decision-maker involved and you should be aware of the 'coalition of clients', which is made up of the following people:

   Feasibility buyer   who is buying the overall idea.

   Technical buyer   who is buying the specialist inputs.

   Financial buyer   who is buying cost-effectiveness.

   Power buyer   who has the right to say 'yes' or 'no'.

   End user   who will make the product work.

   and these are hardly ever the same person.

● Is this a genuine and feasible project? This should be looked at from two points of view, your own and the client's. First, is it a realistic possibility for you? Are you sure it is within your capabilities? Secondly, is it a serious project for the organization or is it just 'something we thought we might do'?

● Is the money available? Find out if the money has already been allocated and which budget it is to be taken from, or if 'we haven't really decided that yet'.

7 Prospective clients may come to meetings with several attitudes towards you. The negative side is the one that makes it clear that the person is suspicious of you and your service; that she is not sure that this 'new' approach would work; and that, whatever it costs, it will be too much. There are those people who are

convinced that consultants borrow your watch, tell you the time and then charge you for the information!

The more positive side, and the one that you will encounter in the majority of cases, comes out in statement like: 'we *must* solve this problem', 'I can't do it by myself', and 'I must tackle this before anyone else in the organization/industry steals my thunder!'

Make a good impression

While you will be watching the way the client behaves during the interview, you can be sure the impression you make on the client will play a large part in whether or not you are asked to do the project.

Ways to make a good impression, as well as making you feel more confident about doing yourself justice, include the following:

- Be prepared – see above.
- Be prompt. The client's first impression should not be of you arriving late, flustered and full of apologies, blaming the traffic, the weather or the dry cleaner who failed to open until 9.30.
- Stay calm and confident. Do not be too modest or self-deprecating but, on the other hand, if you talk about yourself and your achievements too much, you will appear arrogant and brash.
- Do not oversell yourself or your service. If you are able to give evidence to substantiate your claims, such as proof of improved performance in previous assignments, do so, but do not make promises you cannot keep. It is both unethical and illegal.
- Show that you are open-minded and flexible. If you are too dogmatic, the client will not feel convinced that you will be able to view his problems in an objective manner.
- Be good-humoured and cheerful, but do not fall into the trap of behaving like a stand-up comedian, particularly before you are sure of the clients' own sense of humour.
- Dress appropriately for the occasion and the organization you are dealing with. It is generally safer to dress up rather than down until you know more about what is acceptable to the client company. If you would like to know more about which style of clothes and which colours suit you best, contact one of the consultancies, such as **Color Me Beautiful**, (Telephone: 071–627–5211), which specializes in this area. This applies as much to men as to women.

You will, then, need to build marketing and selling into your whole strategy. It is risky to rely on reputation or recommendation alone, especially when you first set up. A good product does not sell itself – it needs some help and you should put aside time to do this. By monitoring the results achieved by different methods, you will build up a picture of the most appropriate channels to use and be able to decide the best mix of marketing approaches to adopt.

13 Health and Self-development

Are you fit for work?

So far we have concentrated on the logistics of setting up as an independent consultant, considering how you will operate, the people you will need to help you, and the way to win business and keep clients. What is missing is a discussion about how you, the person on whom all the activity centres, deals with the pressures that come with this particular life style. Are you fit for work – physically, mentally and professionally? How do you maintain a balance between the different requirements in your life?

I have divided this chapter into three parts:

- personal well-being
- professional self-development
- personal development programmes

We have already mentioned the need to stay up to date with innovations in your field and to build your own self-development into any work programme, but now we go into more depth. First, we shall examine how you look after yourself. Most books which offer advice to people setting up in business leave out the one subject which I feel is fundamental to making a success of what can be a stressful and highly demanding occupation.

Personal well-being

'Stress management' is a common phrase today, but I prefer to think of it in terms of 'personal effectiveness' or 'handling pressure'. The word 'stress' has mainly negative connotations but in truth there are many positive aspects to it. Sportspeople and actors rely on the increased flow of adrenalin to bring out their best performances. Consultants giving important presentations also experience feelings of excitement, nervousness and heightened awareness before and during their performance. They also feel drained and exhausted afterwards. This is all quite normal and should not cause concern. In itself, stress is not harmful, but it is best to avoid unnecessary pressures, to know how to cope with them if they do arise and to recognize the symptoms of too much stress. Handled well, this aspect of your performance can also be of great help to your clients, and forms part of the growing field of 'corporate health'.

Pressures of time

Many people worry about the fact that there are not enough hours in a day, and it may seem even worse if you are a one-person business, having to do everything yourself. Most clients expect consultants to be well-organized and disciplined in their approach to an assignment, prompt in dealing with requests for information and reliable in delivering what they promise. In fact, in my survey, clients rated this skill as the one they considered the most desirable in their consultants. I have written about time management and personal effectiveness in more detail in another book (Garratt, S., 1985, 1990) so I shall not go into it here in great detail. There are, however, some principles to remember.

It is possible to introduce some routine into your work without losing the flexibility that you prize so highly. If done thoughtfully, it will enable you to optimize the time spent on the actual project, doing what you really want to do, rather than worrying about administrative or operational details. You will still have time left over for the other things you value in your life.

In any occupation there are tasks that must be done, those that should be done if possible, and those which would be satisfying or fun to do but which are not essential to the success of the business. If you make a list of jobs to do at the beginning of each week or at the start of a day, this is one of several ways of categorizing what, when and how you should tackle your work.

From the tasks that must be done, identify those which have to be done quickly and those which need some time and thought spent on them. Check that the 'urgent' tasks really do have to be done – I am always intrigued by how many so-called urgent matters do not really need to be attended to until tomorrow and how many actually become obsolete. If anyone tells me that a task is urgent, I try to establish with them an actual time for completion so that I know what the deadline is.

When you have decided which jobs are important and which are urgent, you then allocate the necessary time to them. A good diary or daily planning sheet is useful in helping you give priorities to the demands or your time. It is also worth thinking about the time of day when you work best. Are you at your best early in the morning or during the afternoon? When do you think most clearly, find it easiest to make decisions, and are able to produce good reports and letters? When you have decided which is your best time, try and arrange your work programme around that and leave the routine, less important matters to your least effective part of the day. Some of my colleagues who find it very difficult to wake up in the morning appreciate not having to rush into work early. Your timetable is more flexible when you have control over your day.

One way of reducing the feeling that you have to be working at full speed all day long is to pace yourself and vary the types of task you work on. Do not just rush at everything indiscriminately – pause, put matters into perspective and introduce a change of pace into your work pattern. For example, intersperse the 'heavy' pieces of work with a few routine tasks such as the filing, making some phone calls or treating yourself to a cup of coffee when you have finished a particularly difficult task. One of the great joys of independent consultancy is that you can design each day your way, yet people often feel afraid of such freedom. They begin to behave in ways which are more constraining that those imposed by their old employing organization.

Staying healthy

There are many pressures on consultants to succumb to an unhealthy life style. Invitations to lunch, tight deadlines, worrying about cash flow and future work, fear of refusing projects, and feelings of isolation and helplessness all contribute to stress. You have to recognize where and when stress occurs. Try to identify and write down occasions, people and times that regularly increase your tension. Is it money, deadlines, lack of time, particular people? Just the act of knowing where the problems are helps you to find a solution, an alternative way of doing things.

When you really are under an unreasonable amount of stress, the physical symptoms should alert you to the situation. You may feel tense, have constant headaches or sore throats, suffer from digestive problems, keep going hot and cold, notice that your hands are trembling, and generally not feel well. You may also feel different. You may be aware that you feel panicky, always on the defensive and generally depressed. Your behaviour will change – perhaps you are becoming aggressive, relying on drink, cigarettes or drugs to calm you down, and you may have become accident prone.

All of these signs mean that you have to stand back and take stock of the situation, and take the necessary steps towards a healthier way of living. Except for extreme medical cases, you may be able to heal yourself with some simple resolutions. For example:

- Eat sensibly, exercise properly and rest well – then you will be in a better position to fight off the negative aspects of stress.

    It is tempting to keep on working if you are busy and not have breaks for lunch or a mid-morning cup of coffee. Part of pacing yourself properly is to know when to take breaks to rest your brain, to move your limbs and have a change of surroundings. Taking lunch does not place you under an obligation to stop for a full hour or to eat an enormous meal washed down with alcohol. Moderation in the middle of the working day is a wise policy, particularly if you are with clients. I very much dislike the 'working lunch' (or breakfast or dinner come to that); I am sure that asking the brain and digestion to work at full speed at the same time leads to indigestion of both head and gut, and underperformance in both.

    Some kind of exercise is beneficial to everyone. This does not mean rushing to the squash court once every six months to prove that you are still young and active. I have often seen delegates at a conference jogging painfully round the grounds of the hotel and hear them admit that they have never done it before or only when they are away from home. Exercise should be regular, within your capabilities, and you should always warm up and warm down before and after any physical activity. Much serious illness among busy people is due to irregular strenuous exercise without preparing the body adequately for the unaccustomed exertion. It is also true that the combination of rich food, excessive alcohol and too much/too little exercise can be dangerous, if not fatal.

The body needs rest as well as exercise if the correct balance is to be maintained. Some people need more sleep than others but, however long you need, make sure that you have enough. There will always be times when a deadline means you have to work extremely hard for a few days, and this may result in only a few hours' sleep each night during that period. The body can easily cope with this if you are fit, but it will react badly if it becomes a regular occurrence.

- Have regular check-ups. This is particularly important as you get older or have a history of illness. If you object in principle to belonging to one of the private health schemes, your doctor will be pleased to give you a general examination to test that everything is in working order.

  In addition to modern medicine, you may wish to consult practitioners of complementary or alternative medicine. For example, if you suffer from back pain, you are as likely to find relief from a chiropractor as from a doctor. If you are aware that the nature of your work places unnecessary stresses on your body, for instance if you are a designer standing at your drawing board for long periods at a time, you might consider learning the Alexander Technique which teaches you how to 'fine tune' your body, how to bring it back into balance. To what extent you use these complementary methods will depend on your own beliefs.

- Learn to relax. Take regular bouts of proper relaxation and build them into your day. This is a time for deep unwinding, not just five minutes sitting on your desk with a cup of tea. You can learn how to meditate or you can devote time to a personal way of relaxing such as walking, music or sport. The time set aside for this must be inviolable – and must not be the first thing to be sacrificed as soon as work builds up.

The office

For people who have not been used to running an office or doing all the administrative work themselves, the new routines and details may prove a source of stress. For an office to provide a sound support for you and your work, it is worth spending time setting up the systems which will actually help you and not just create a source of frustration. Much of the equipment which will make your job easier is described in Chapter 7. If you really hate office work but cannot afford any help yet, arrange a routine so that you do the filing, type up the invoices, update the accounts and check the stationery supplies regularly and efficiently. In that way you will spend as little time as is necessary on these tasks. They have to be done and you can get yourself into all sorts of trouble, operational and legal, if they are neglected.

I would emphasize again the importance of the design of your workplace, particularly in relation to the way it affects you physically. An office should be well ventilated but not too cold. Also, if you have computers and photocopiers in a smallish space, do not allow them to overheat.

Many people who operate computer keyboards have not learned to type on a traditional typewriter. While this does not affect their ability to operate the machine, it may mean that they do not know how to sit properly, or understand where their hands and arms should be in relation to the keyboard. There are increasing numbers of cases of repetitive strain injury (RSI) being reported among people who use keyboards often. This is a very painful inflammation of the joints, usually the wrists, elbows and up to the shoulders and necks in serious cases. It occurs through repeating a particular action over a long period of time, and when it first appears many patients and doctors think it is rheumatism. For anyone who uses a keyboard, the advice is to make sure you take regular breaks, not only from straining your eyes looking at the screen, but also from repeating the action of striking the keys. Stop every twenty minutes or so and do something else for a short while. In extreme cases, sufferers may not regain the full use of their hands if they do not heed the first warning pains.

Another common factor in RSI cases is that keyboards are often too high in front of the operator. Ideally, your shoulders should be down and your hands and elbows should be in a straight line, parallel to the floor and level with the keyboard.

I do not like most of the chairs that have supposedly been designed specially for keyboard operators. Many of them lack proper back support and the seats are so designed that the upper part of your leg slopes upwards from hip to knee instead of slightly downwards. You should be able to place your feet firmly on the floor and keep your whole body in balance without placing stress on any part. Chairs with no backs and those which you grip with your knees do not fulfil these criteria. An architect friend, who knows I have a weak back and also that I have to spend a great deal of time at a typewriter or computer keyboard, asked if I would try out a chair he had designed and built. He would be the first to agree that it is not the most beautiful chair in the world but it has made a great improvement to my working life.

Travelling

As traffic gets denser, roads more crowded and rush hours seem to last all day, travelling becomes a stressful activity for many people. In town and city centres, using a car may be a nightmare, particularly as it is usually difficult to find parking spaces. In more isolated areas, where public transport is unreliable, a car may be the only plausible way to get about.

We have managed without a car for over fifteen years, but we can only do that because we are based near good bus routes and central London railway stations and we have access to a reliable minicab service. Travelling round the United Kingdom means that we rely on trains and planes, taking taxis, and hiring a car at the other end if appropriate and, on the whole we find this works very well. We have built up a long list of reliable taxi firms all over the United Kingdom. This arrangement will not suit everyone, nor will it be a feasible proposition for others, but it may be worth considering letting someone else do the driving. I also appreciate the opportunity to prepare to meet the client, catch up on reading or even some sleep on the train, and feel sorry for my colleagues who are caught in traffic jams and suffering the stress of having to concentrate so completely for long periods of unproductive time.

If you have to travel long distances by car, give yourself plenty of time for the journey, allowing for short stops for refreshments and perhaps some simple exercises to loosen stiff limbs and to keep you alert. It is advisable to keep the car well ventilated, because too warm an atmosphere can make you drowsy. We always try to prepare for any car journey by working out at least two routes in case there are any problems with the first choice.

What does surprise me is how many consultants' cars add to the physical stress placed on the body. For example, many people have backache but choose low-slung cars which cause terrific back strain just getting in and out. The driving seat is often set so that the driver can lie back 'to be more comfortable on long journeys'. This is nonsense. The human head weighs about 14lb and pivots from a line between the ears, not at the back of the neck as many think. This mean that the head needs to be upright, and this in turn means that the back also needs to be upright, so the seat should be vertical. The arms should be slightly stretched and the legs tilted slightly downwards. In most cars, this is almost impossible to achieve but there are 'travel wedges' now available to help alleviate this. Such a driving position will feel odd at first – unless you have one of the 'Espace' or 'Prairie' types which makes it seem a little easier – but it is worth persevering with it as the reduction in stress during driving – and hence, the ability to arrive fresh to do the client's work or back home to 're-charge your batteries' – is noticeable. An Alexander Technique teacher will be able to advise on the best way to deal with posture when travelling.

When travelling by train we always arrange to be met at the destination by a local taxi firm or by the organization or hotel where we will be based. Again, checking times and possible hold-ups, such as engineering works beforehand keeps down the risks.

Long-distance flights bring their own stresses. I find it difficult to believe anyone who says 'I don't suffer from jet lag'. It is possible to minimize the effects, but travelling for, say, twelve hours to the Far East and experiencing a time difference of eight hours is bound to make you feel somewhat disorientated. Doctors say it takes one day to adjust to each hour of time difference. Many multinational corporations will not let their executives take any decision within forty-eight hours of arriving after a long-haul flight.

I am always amazed at how some of my fellow travellers behave. They drink vast amounts of alcohol – spirits, wine and digestifs – and eat everything that is put in front of them. Although the airlines are proud of their food and wine lists, many of them now suggest that you should not overindulge. It is easy to dehydrate in an aircraft and the consumption of alcohol only adds to the problem. It may be more boring to drink just fruit juices or water but it is healthier. It is also important to exercise from time to time. Wriggling your wrists and ankles and stretching your arms and legs will keep your circulation moving and lessen the risks of swollen ankles or, at worst, blood clots. Always wear comfortable, loose-fitting clothes – even in First Class! You can change at the other end or just before you land.

If you are travelling a long way abroad for business, and particularly if you need to be on top form at the other end, try to arrange your flight so that you arrive with a couple of days to spare. You have to feel comfortable with your surroundings and confident that you have access to the resources you need, so the extra time will help you acclimatize. When travelling somewhere for the first time, do your homework before you go, so that you are sure you are as prepared as possible for an unaccustomed climate, unfamiliar food, unknown social customs and different business conventions. We helped to produce a training package, 'China Business Briefing' for business people thinking about setting up in China, and a great deal of the accompanying book was about culture, customs, history, political and economic structure, food, climate and so on. Thorough preparation is rarely wasted in any situation. Find out what your clients' policies are about arriving early and acclimatizing – there are enlightened clients about!

I have to admit that one of my dislikes is the mobile telephone but I am sure that they can reduce stress, both for consultants and clients, in certain circumstances. For instance, if you are going to be late for a meeting, it is useful to be able to ring the clients from a car, taxi, train, or motorway hard shoulder, and let them know what is happening. They may not like it, but they will be able to adjust their timetable accordingly.

Be fit for life – maintaining the balance

One way to minimize the negative aspects of stress is to strike the right personal balance between work, home and leisure. This balance will be different for every individual and may change during the various phases of your life, so it is worth reviewing your priorities from time to time.

During your first two or three years as an independent operator, you will probably be tempted to become totally immersed in your work. It is at this time that even the most understanding partners and friends will find that their patience is sorely tested. Most people will recognize your need to build up the business, but your true friends will also persuade you to honour your holiday commitments, join the local tennis club or take up photography – or anything that will help you keep work in perspective. Most importantly, discuss what is happening with the people with whom you are most deeply involved. Any change, and particularly one like this where your whole life style is altered, can have a profound effect on those you live with, as well as on you. Even as simple a change as putting in a business phone line at home can help relieve the pressure of and on the family – especially if you have teenage children!

Working from home means that it is sometimes difficult to separate business time from social and domestic time. The wife of one of my colleagues became so annoyed with the way he would sneak into his office when they were supposed to be on holiday, that she pinned a large notice on the office door that read 'Out of Bounds to David until 28 August'. The first time he saw it he stopped dead in his tracks and then, realizing the effect his actions were having on everybody else, he stayed out of the office until the end of the holiday.

Professional self-development

In a recent study on consultants (GMS Consultancy, 1990), it was found that many freelances have not taken any training since they became independent. This was due as much to the low quality and high cost of much training as to the consultant's unwillingness to undergo more training. However, the report concluded that 'the prosperous operators are those who keep technical and business skills up to date'.

Just as the lowest form of life has to adapt to changes in its surroundings if it is to survive, so too must all other organisms, whether a plant in the meadow, a multinational corporation or even an independent consultant. This truth was succinctly expressed by Reg Revans (1982) in the formula $L \geqslant C$: that is, in order to survive, the rate of learning of any organism has to be equal to, or greater than the rate of change in its environment. In the present climate, as the number of independent operators is growing, your ability to adapt and move forward will determine your chances of success.

Your professional self-development will probably include some training and a number of other aspects. Self-development means constantly broadening your knowledge and skills, giving yourself new challenges and goals, testing your abilities and ideas, and keeping up to date with what is going on in your subject area and in the world around you.

For some of these activities, you will need to make a conscious effort, while others may become part of your everyday life and routine. A first step would be to make sure you read at least one quality newspaper each day in order to gain a broad picture of national and international affairs. A journal such as *The Economist* or, if you are interested in a particular part of the world, a publication similar to *Far East Economic Review* or *Wall Street Journal*, will go into more detail. Magazines related to your profession will be obligatory reading anyway, but if you are, for example, an architect, the *Architect's Journal* might be complemented by *Blueprint* to give a broader view of the design world.

Some consultants feel that they can become rather isolated when they are not working directly with clients, yet they do not think they can legitimately spend time away from the office. One perfectly acceptable way of overcoming this isolation while, at the same time, developing yourself, is to become an active member of the associations you have joined. Attend their meetings, talk to as many interesting people as you can and listen to and contribute to the latest ideas and views in your field. The Association for Management Education and Development, for instance, runs regular sessions where members explain and exchange their latest ideas and examples of 'best practice', enjoying lively debates in the process. This is also a way of testing yourself against peers you respect and from whom you can learn.

Other ways of testing yourself are by writing books and articles, lecturing or running workshops. These will be for a different audience from those you will address wearing your marketing hat. Here your aim is not to impress potential clients but to gain opinions from colleagues and friends. From this input, you will be able to sharpen your thoughts to practical ways of working.

Training, or the acquisition of skills, will be more appropriate for some consultants than others as they begin their independent careers, and the subject matter will vary. For example, a film-maker whose previous experience was with a television company may not have received any formal interpersonal skills training. He will have learned a great deal from experience but may now wish to perfect the ability to work in harmony with clients. Different techniques of handling people in all kinds of situations will prove invaluable, and there are many good courses on the market. A designer who has plenty of experience in scheduling projects may have little idea of budgeting or other financial matters and would benefit from a 'Finance for Non-Financial Managers' course. An accountant may be a wizard with numbers but could do with some help on running meetings, and a legal adviser would find a course on how to produce visual aids most useful.

All of this again emphasizes that you must be aware of the skills and knowledge you have *and* what you still need in order to become more effective as a consultant. When you first start off as an independent operator, I have suggested that you make an inventory of skills and qualities. This is not just a one-off exercise. It should be something you do on a regular basis, always bearing in mind your growing experience and your evolving market. Among the aspects to consider are the following:

● If you are not receiving assignments after submitting proposals or meeting prospective clients, try to find out why. If it is because of the quality of your presentation or limited knowledge of a subject, you will be able to note those down as areas that you can quickly brush up on. If you fail because of fee structure or too much competition, go back to your marketing plan.

● Watch other consultants in action. Go to conferences and meetings where you can observe their strengths and notice what could be improved. This does not, of course, mean that you should just imitate them, but it will give you ideas for modifying your own behaviour and approach. I often admire those consultants who give performances of Olivier-type proportions when working with clients. They are sometimes quite outrageous in a way that I know I could never confidently be, but they succeed in their performances. I realize that my temperament will not allow me to be quite so extrovert, but it does encourage me to be a little more adventurous when the occasion allows.

Personal development programme

Many of the more enlightened organizations are introducing the idea of 'personal development agreements' for their employees. In these cases, the agreement is between the company and the individual, but you could adapt the idea for your position as both company *and* employee! The idea is that, in return for attaining agreed targets of performance and behaviour, employees will be entitled to a certain amount of time and money to stretch themselves by undertaking a personal development programme. This can include acquiring new skills (not necessarily related to the organization's business), enrolling for some form of distance learning or improving an aspect of physical fitness. This encourages individuals to take responsibility for their own development and it can easily be applied to independent operators, too.

Draw up a list of 'resolutions'. For example, during the next twelve months I will:

1   earn fees of at least £40,000;
2   work for at least three new clients;
3   take at least three weeks' holiday;
4   create a workable filing system;
5   learn to use the database on the computer
6   mend the broken relationship with the local printer (because he's the best, nearest and cheapest); and
7   write an article for my professional institute's magazine

and when I have attained each of these, I promise I will allow myself to:

1   go to the Annual Conference in Rome;
2   join the local leisure centre;
3   enrol for a counselling skills course; and
4   buy a new car for the family

The need to make your practice successful means that you may sacrifice parts of your life to the idea that 'I must take on as much work as I can for the first couple of years'. If this is taken to an extreme, your health and relationships with others will suffer, sometimes irreparably. Try to maintain the right balance for the circumstances. As you grow more confident in your abilities, you will be able to make choices about how you spend your time, energies and money, more easily. When you have that degree of control, you will be both 'fit for work' and 'fit for life'.

Use this page to draw up your own personal development programme when you are ready to do so.

Within the next ☐ months, I will:	Then I will allow myself to:
1	
2	
3	
4	
5	
6	
7	
8	
9	
10	

14 Looking Ahead

Many of the areas we have discussed so far – what you have to offer, how you will organize yourself and your business, who you will need to advise you, how to improve basic management skills, how to market and sell yourself, how to monitor the external world, how to stay healthy and fit for work – will also be useful in making the future less risky. In addition, you will need to define a strategy for your business. You will have a vision which shows you not only what you would like the future to hold for you, but also how you will achieve your aims.

The personal development programme (see Chapter 13) will be part of this and it may be useful to examine other ways of gathering and analysing data to help you look forward and cope with the changing market.

This chapter suggests two ways of monitoring the environment – known by the acronyms PPEST and SWOT. They provide a framework by means of which you can keep a regular and rigorous check on what is happening out there and what you need to do to keep up with events. They enable you to spot any gaps in skills and knowledge and to act on this information, so that you are abreast of new developments and not trailing along several months behind. Once established, these frameworks are easy to update and maintain.

There is also a section on the increasingly important and relevant area of intellectual property rights. An awareness of how you can protect your ideas and products and make sure that they will not be stolen and used by other people, as well as understanding how much you may or may not use other's materials, will become more significant in the future.

The final section of this chapter includes the opportunity for you to look ahead and set the criteria by which you will be able to recognize your success when it comes. These benchmarks enable you to judge how well or how badly you are doing, and to modify your way of working accordingly. If you do not stop to review performance from time to time, it is likely that you will waste precious time and energy.

How, then, do you start monitoring the environment in which you are operating?

PPEST

This stands for:

- Political changes
- Physical environment changes
- Economic changes
- Social changes
- Technological changes

Much of the required information can be gained from newspapers and journals. By creating a database from cuttings and articles, you will be able to stay aware of all changes which touch upon your sphere of work and interests. This data may be kept in folders on your desk, or held in your computer or on a library database – it does not really matter as long as you keep to the discipline of collecting the information and reviewing it on a regular basis.

Discuss and debate these issues regularly with colleagues and professional or social contacts in order to broaden your knowledge and understanding. After a few months, you will find that you read newspapers and watch TV with a much more constructive attitude – one that keeps you up to date and often ahead of your competitors.

On each issue ask yourself the following questions: 'What does this mean for my existing/potential clients?' and 'What does this mean for me?' Compile your own list, for example, as follows:

Issue	Clients	Me

1 *Political changes*

- Consequences of competition policy in local authorities

- 1992 and after in the European Community

- Possibility of a change of government after the next election

2 *Physical environment changes*

- Reduction in the use of chlorofluorocarbons (CFCs)

- Greater emphasis on quality of health at work/generally

- Global warming's effect on population distribution

3 *Economic changes*

- Growth of decentralized organizations

- European monetary unions

- Growth of trading blocs in Europe/ US/Japan

- Energy taxes replacing people taxes

4 *Social changes*

- Demographic changes in the population

- Growth in new forms of working

- Implosion of middle management

- Learning becoming increasingly important as a key organizational asset

- Tele-commuting

5 *Technological changes*

- Expert systems development/ artificial intelligence
- Interactive information systems development
- Hybrid diesel/electric cars becoming available

SWOT

This means:

Strengths + Weaknesses = internal

Opportunities + Threats = external

It is useful to carry out a SWOT analysis of your consultancy on a quarterly basis, preferably using a group of colleagues as a sounding board, and incorporating all the data you have collected, together with past experiences.

Compile your list, for example, as follows:

1 *Strengths*

• professional expertise	(list)
• strong client base	(list)
• reasonable asset base	(list)

2 *Weaknesses*

• no foreign languages	(list)
• poor public speaking skills	(examples)
• little family support	(examples)
• highly fluctuating cashflow	

3   *Opportunities*

- significant changes in large organizations   (list)
  (using the PPEST analysis)

4   *Threats*

- substantial/increasing competition in
  following areas:

- change of tax status for independent
  consultant

Throughout this book, I have stressed the need to be aware of the new developments relating to your area of work. It should be as if you have super-delicate antennae which are forever probing and sensitive to what is happening around you, picking up information that will affect your life and your work.

Intellectual property

Part of your plan for the future should be to make it your business to find out what is new in all aspects of your sphere of operation. Some changes and developments in various areas may have profound effects on your work. One important area is that of 'intellectual property', and I have therefore included a section on this subject, examining how it might affect your work as a consultant.

Many independent consultant become so involved with the process of consulting that they lose sight of the physical outputs created by their consulting. So what, you may ask? Well, you may be forfeiting the intrinsic and extrinsic rewards of the things you create, but do not bother to codify and register. At the highest level, there is the personal satisfaction of having created a unique artefact. At the lowest level, there is the concern that others have stolen your idea and, what is worse, are making money from it.

The content and processes of your consultancy service are an intellectual activity. The physical outputs are intellectual property. This is becoming, in an information-based society, a tradeable commodity. Some would argue that in the twenty-first century it will be *the* tradeable asset of a business – organizations will survive or die simply on their ability to learn and turn that learning into a product or service, that is, something the customers want. The importance of the L ⩾ C argument is again emphasized (see page 128).

To be able to secure your product or service, it is necessary to create a legal right over it, hence the term 'intellectual property rights' (IPRS) which is an esoteric but very fast-growing area of national, EC and international law. It will affect you one way or another – through enabling you to create your own rights and having the option of charging people to use them; or by having to pay others for permission to use their material; or through having to sue others who are illegally using your material. The area of IPRs is likely to make a significant impact on the costing and pricing processes of consultancy in the twenty-first century.

What are intellectual property rights?

There are five main categories accepted in most countries:

- Patent
- Copyright
- Registered design
- Trademark
- Servicemark

Patent is the one familiar to most people. It operates on the principle that, if you can show, through drawings, formulae and other physical manifestations, that you have an idea for a unique product or a unique development of a product, then, after a due legal search and registration process, you will be granted the right to manufacture, use or allow others to use this exclusive design under your patent. It is a slow and very costly process and needs to be undertaken in each country separately (although the EC hopes to change this within its boundaries). Unless you are consulting in the design industry or biochemistry and pharmaceuticals industries (the patenting of genes is a debatable recent development), most consultants are more likely to use patented equipment than to have to patent it themselves. The area is so complicated from a legal viewpoint that the advice of a patent agent should be sought immediately you have a query.

Copyright is much easier to understand and much less easy to enforce. In the United Kingdom, copyright exists in any writing/ drawing as soon as it is created. However, if you write or draw something which is unique to you and you wish to make it clear that you own the property, you will reinforce the fact by the simple process of writing, at the end of each page or the whole, ©, your name and the year. Should someone else want to use or copy this, they will then be obliged to consult you, and it is for you to agree the terms under which they must do so. There are obvious problems in enforcing this, and most people have worked for years on the crude principle that if you alter something by 20 per cent or more then you are likely to be clear of any copyright liability. However, times are changing and recently large sums have changed hands mainly in out-of-court settlements, in cases where, for example, a management consultancy was illegally copying psychometric tests and using them in a client company. As the client was also named in the threatened action, this did nothing for the consultancy's continued good relations with that client.

Copyright applies *inter alia* to books, papers, worksheets, diagrams, schedules and timelogs, so it is worth assessing not only the obvious output of your consultancy, but also the back-up software to see just what you have codified and to consider what you have created that might be of use to others.

Registered design is similar in some ways to copyright but refers specifically to physical designs of artefacts which are not patentable, that is, they are developments of existing items such as chairs, tables, lamps and so on which may well use patentable elements which are reinterpretations on an existing theme. Like copyright, this is a difficult area to enforce, but an increasingly important one as the multinationals fight for global brands. One example is the fight by Toblerone over the design of their triangular chocolate bars. They considered it worth pursuing a multimillion dollar court case to protect their intellectual property in the design.

Trademark is a well-known symbol. The ⓉⓂ beside a well-known brand or manufacturer's name shows that the product or service has been registered under that name and that no one else has permission to use the name and style without explicit permission. Unless trademarking is handled well, it can lead to embarrassing and expensive problems for consultants and companies alike. Some sharp people around the world make a good living registering company names, brand names and trademarks in small to medium-sized countries before the lawyers of big corporations get round to doing it. They then sell back these rights at extortionate rates! And it is not just the big corporations that suffer. In a Far Eastern country this year, I found that a UK professional institute, a branch of which I wished to establish there, had had its name, and combinations of the words in its title, registered some time previously. To get access to what we thought was our 'rightful' name, we had to buy it back. This kind of situation can have interesting implications for the registration of your consultancy name overseas.

Servicemark is a new idea and symbol, (SM) , which is developing as the service industries grow. It is a type of branding of a service rather than a specific product. It is a way of differentiating your service from others in what might otherwise be seen as a simple commodity. For example. all banks now have cash machines as a necessary customer service. These are differentiated by the names each bank gives to its ATM (Automated Teller Machine), for example, 'Speedlink' or 'Servicetill'. These are the services on which a servicemark can be created.

Most of this may sound a long way away from independent consultants. Increasingly, this will not be so. Commercially-minded people are seeing the area of IPRs as a good way of giving competitive advantage to their organizations and the law is changing to help them. You will increasingly have to see this as a consideration on your SWOT analysis (see page 138). To give some idea of the scale at the upper end of the IPR arena, Thorn–EMI, which owns the IPRs to thousands of songs, recently revalued its balance sheet and added in its IPRs for the first time. This added £3.5 billion to its assets!

Two last points on IPRs. First, this is such a complex and rapidly developing area of law that you need good professional legal advice on it if you are to enter it at all. Do not use a general jobbing lawyer but a firm with an IPR department or specialist. There are not yet many lawyers with significant experience in this field.

Second, some people find this whole area distasteful, even unethical. Like the Chinese, they cry 'There should be no tax on knowledge'. People who sympathize with this view fear that the rise of IPRs will challenge some of the fundamental tenets of behaviour in, for example, science. The need to publish and debate freely has always been a feature of the international scientific community, but will this continue to be so if universities or sponsors are keen to keep new developments secret until IPRs are established over them? The growing area of IPR laws could drive an ethical wedge between theory and practice. Many people are, theoretically, on the side of open publication, but are not sure how they would behave in practice if someone blatantly stole their ideas and products. A compromise might be to register them so that the owner is in control of who has free use of them and who pays for them.

How do you know when you're successful?

My final thoughts on setting up on your own are about how you judge your performance and know that you are a successful independent consultant.

When you talk of wanting to be successful, or admire someone else for being successful, what do you mean? What in your eyes constitutes success and, if you do not meet those criteria, are you necessarily a failure?

I remember one occasion when Bob Garratt and I spoke to a group of people who were only just starting up as independent consultants. They were very quiet at first and when we asked them why, the general opinion was that they were intimidated by us because we were so obviously successful. 'What', we then asked 'makes you think that we are successful?' The answers varied: 'you look prosperous'; 'you look and sound confident'; 'you are self-assured, even with an audience you've never met before'; 'you speak with authority'; 'you're relaxed enough to joke with us'; 'you're good listeners'. This provided a good starting point for our discussions.

I am sure it's important to think about 'success', particularly as, during the times when things are not going to plan, the over-pessimistic may be ready to give it all up, while the over-optimistic will pretend it is just a temporary problem and smile bravely all the way to insolvency.

Does success for you mean:

1   having enough money to cover all outgoings and:

- run two cars?
- educate the children privately?
- have two holidays a year?
- have a second home in Norfolk/Wales/France?
- wear designer clothes?

2   being able to play golf once a week?

3   becoming a 'personality' on TV?
4   being asked to give after-dinner speeches or keynote addresses?

When you think of people you regard as successful, is it because they seem to have plenty of money, to be always working, to be content with their lot, to be happy in their personal relationships? Are these the things that you want?

It is good to set yourself high standards and realistic goals, but dangerous to become obsessed with always getting things right. When trying out new ideas or techniques, conducting courses or running projects, you can minimize risks by preparation and forethought, but you will never be able to eliminate all the mistakes or anticipate every unscheduled happening. When the unexpected does happen – pause, see how or if it changes the situation, and act accordingly. You may have to make a decision immediately or you may have time to reflect or discuss matters with other people.

If a project did not turn out to be the overwhelming success you had hoped for, do not despair. Much can be learned from mistakes. Our first instinct is often to blame somebody else, everybody else. If you resist that urge, you may gain some useful hints from a review of the project. You might find it helpful to write a short report, for your personal attention only, at the end of each assignment, giving details of what went well, what you would do differently another time and what should be abandoned for future occasions. Do not think of something that was not an obvious success as an outright failure. It may teach you some valuable lessons about how to approach future work, how to behave with clients and how to run your business – which is, I think, where we came in.

Success means something different to each of us. Part of me would love to be very rich, but that would require doing a different type of work which I know I would not enjoy. In addition to working longer hours, it would also mean giving up playing tennis a couple of times a week, having fewer dinner parties and not entertaining my god-children so often. At this stage in my life, those pursuits are too important to give up, so I will postpone the idea of that world cruise for now. Perhaps I will fit it in later . . . unless something more attractive comes along.

I hope that this book helps you to achieve your aims and that you enjoy being a consultant. I hope it also helps you to avoid some of the pitfalls. More positively, I trust it will help you to face your first

few years with confidence and optimism, well prepared to take
calculated risks. Above all, I hope you will have fun and personal
development, for that is the essential aspect of being an independent
consultant. Are you ready for the challenge?

Final thoughts

I asked several consultants what was the best piece of advice they
had ever been given as they started their lives as independent
operators. Some of the answers given were as follows:

- 'Don't panic when you don't have any work.'
- 'Keep your face and name in people's minds.'
- 'There is no such thing as failure, only feedback.'
- 'If people criticize you, always listen, don't defend – it will usually
  give you some insight.'
- 'Don't take everything that floats past – I ignored that piece of
  advice for twelve months and nearly died of exhaustion!'
- 'Don't overtrade.'
- 'Maintain a balance between work and home.'
- 'Stick your neck out a bit further – have more confidence in
  yourself – sell yourself a bit more.'
- 'Don't go out on your own too early. I would have liked to
  become independent ten years ago but I know I wouldn't have
  had the experience or skill.'
- 'You are happy while the telephone keeps ringing. The first time
  it doesn't, you panic. There is a pattern and you have to learn to
  take the quiet times and use them. The pendulum will swing back.
  Quiet moments are for making contacts, reading, sitting back and
  developing new ideas.'

Appendix

Professional Liability and Indemnity Insurance

by Susan Hay

Professional responsibility

Public expectation

The whole business of becoming a consultant is open to abuse. There is no law which prevents virtually anyone setting up and offering consultancy services of almost any kind. There are, however, legal restrictions on what you call yourself. Although you might offer architectural services, for example, you have to be a qualified and registered architect before you may call yourself an architect. You may call yourself an accountant but not a chartered accountant, unless you are a member of one of the Institutes of Chartered Accountants.

What matters in law is that you do not present yourself to the public as someone you are not. They must not be led to expect more than you can deliver. What is more, your competence will be judged against the service you are purporting to offer. If you convey to a client that you are a surveyor, the client is entitled to expect a level of competence and skills similar to that of a chartered surveyor.

It is clearly a good deal easier to determine use or abuse of an image when dealing with a traditional discipline than when the situation involves, for instance, a management consultant or a computer consultant, where the client who had been wronged would not have the benefit of a standard qualification system or an established code of professional conduct to refer to as a measure of competence.

Each work opportunity carries with it a degree of risk. The risk, apart from financial, is to do with whether or not you do the work to the satisfaction of your client. Have you done what you said you would do to the standard to which they are entitled? This is the liability you carry as a consultant. The risks involved need to be identified and then managed. Any part of the risk which is beyond your own control should be transferred to an insurer.

Members of a profession are, or should be, distinctive, because they live by a set of rules designed to protect not only themselves but also the public. They know and act upon the knowledge that incompetence or wrongdoing on the part of one of their members will colour the public's perception of them all. All over the world, the last quarter of a century has become the era of the consumer. Educational, social, economic and political pressures have tended to mould public opinion to seek a fair deal for the consumer, and judgements held in the courts have mirrored this. The public now thinks in absolutes; having sought and obtained advice or assistance, it is expected that the service is so perfect as to constitute an absolute guarantee. This expectation applies to all professions, but allowances are made for some and not others. The doctor's patient expects medical treatment to be correct but most of us accept that medical science has not yet charted all the byways of the physical and mental human conditions. We know that in a court action there has to be a winning lawyer and one who loses. Accountancy and engineering are, on the other hand, seen to be more exact skills.

Liability is derived from the responsibility and trust you ask your clients to place in you. They select you carefully and, having been given a commission, you do not expect them to doubt your ability to carry out the work.

As a consumer, if you are not satisfied with a can of baked beans, you buy another brand next time. Not so when you buy the services of a consultant. You may only do it once or twice in your life, and if it all goes wrong, or even if you are a bit disappointed at the outcome you are horrified and are very likely to resolve never to do it again! How many of us have criticized doctors for not being able to tell us what is wrong with us? We have probably only had experience of one or two, but as far as we are concerned the entire profession is tarnished!

'All professionals are a conspiracy against the laity', said Bernard Shaw. He was talking about winning the public's trust and then abusing it. He was also speaking in the days before it was common practice to seek compensation from the consultant who had wronged you.

'Risk' and its management has become a business in its own right because we, the members of the consuming public, are no longer prepared to blame ourselves for careless or negligent behaviour on the part of those who provide us with a service. An example of this would be us making a mistake in our choice of consultant.

Legal climate

Why is everyone so concerned about their liability exposure at the moment?

First, the legal rules of liability have changed. Society has become litigious. Every man and woman is now conscious that if they have been treated in some way which falls short of what they were led to expect, they can sue. There will be no shortage of solicitors, barristers and expert witnesses to help them. They can also sue their lawyer!

Legislation in the United Kingdom is becoming more complex and broader in its approach as more statutes arise out of comprehensive European directives. During the latter part of the 1980s, there was a flurry of new statutes, each of mammoth proportions: the Insolvency Act, the Latent Damage Act, the Financial Services Act and the Consumer Protection Act.

Gradually the consumer has learnt that the terms of their agreement with a professional adviser do not impose an absolute limit on the ability to bring an action; claims can be made in contract and in tort (negligence). While an action in tort is not within the control of the individual citizen, an action in contract basically is, and this fact is being considered in the way commissioning arrangements between client and consultant are interpreted. The terms of your commission with a client form the first line of potential 'damage limitation'. If terms are not expressly set out, it is open to either party to suggest that some duties which have not been fulfilled should have been. If a breach of contract occurs because the consultant has failed to exercise the standard of professional skill which is implied in that contract, even if it is not expressly stated, then the injured party has a period of six years from the date of the breach in which to bring proceedings.

The legal principle of negligence (tort) is that we all owe a duty of care to our 'neighbour'. This means anyone who is reasonably within our contemplation. There are three essential prerequisites for a claim of negligence to be established:

- that a duty is owed to the plaintiff by the defendant;
- that the duty has been breached; and
- that the plaintiff has suffered damage as a result of the breach.

The period in which claims may be brought is similarly six years. However, this requires some qualification. Until the passing of the Latent Damage Act in 1986, the decision in *Pirelli* v. *Oscar Faber & Partners* settled the law to the extent that the cause of action accrued at the date the damage occurred, even where the plaintiff was ignorant that damage had occurred. The Act states that there is now a period 'of three years for the action to be brought from the date when the damage is discovered or could reasonably have been discovered, provided that no cause of action shall lie more than fifteen years from the date of the defendant's breach of duty'.

In the general view, the Latent Damage Act does little to clarify the period for which a professional remains liable. It is argued that both the plaintiff who has suffered loss and needs to be certain of proper compensation, and the consultant whose insurers must be able to calculate the real extent of their professional indemnity risk, are still left confused and uncertain of their respective limits. At the time of writing, the new Act remains untested.

Emerging professions such as management consultants and computer consultants pose new problems in identifying liabilities and assessing risk. These new professions are not generally as formally organized as the traditional professions and do not operate on a corporate basis. They do not have influential institutions supporting them and furthering their interests; they have little regulation or monitoring of their conduct. Their businesses tend to be much more individualistic.

It is clear that a client, in attempting to claim damages from a consultant, could first look to the commissioning arrangement between them to see if any of its terms had been breached; second, s/he could consider whether the consultant had acted without due care and skill and had been negligent; third, if the consultant had been sufficiently involved in the decisions which the client had taken and which had resulted in loss, they might consider whether a criminal action under the Insolvency Act 1985 could be brought.

Case law shows that fundamental differences exist between various types of consultant as far as liability is concerned, as follows:

- those who are generally expected to achieve material success (architects, engineers, solicitors doing non-contentious work) and those who are not (doctors, litigating solicitors);
- those who generally do not have contracts with their clients (doctors, barristers) and those who do (accountants, management consultants, architects);
- hierarchical professions (medicine, the bar) and those which are not so formally structured (solicitors, architects, management consultants).

The courts can set standards by which consultants are judged but they cannot set the standards which they must achieve. This must be done by the consultants themselves and is largely why expert witnesses have become increasingly required in cases involving technical expertise.

Managing responsibilities

The hazards associated with becoming a consultant are numerous. They exist as soon as it is decided to initiate a project, and continue to flourish throughout its duration. The important step is to identify risk, because it is only by perceiving that it exists that its probability and severity can be reduced, using the formula: or –

$$\text{risk} = \text{severity of hazard} \times \text{probability of occurrence}$$

Risk assessment is critical if the consultant is to be provided with a reasonable method of measuring the gains and losses of a complex course of action. Such assessment will lead to a calculated risk, with known odds of success or failure. Of course, these odds may be unacceptable and the course of action then rejected. Alternatively, a method may be found to improve the odds. When risks are identified, they need to be allocated to the various parties involved in the project. The most appropriate method may be to do so on the basis of control over their occurrence and their effect when they materialize. The following should be considered:

- the risk, its level and extent;
- the arrangement for dealing with the hazard if and when it materializes, and;
- the situation connected with the hazard.

The party which has control should accept the risk.

Generally speaking, if risks give rise to loss or damages, as they are bound to do, then disputes will arise over liability for the cost of such loss. If responsibilities and liabilities have been clearly established, the surest way of guarding against any future loss and limiting its effect is through insurance.

Reducing liability

One effect of the massive increases in the cost of professional indemnity insurance premiums in recent years is that consultants have been forced to give greater attention to the risks they face.

Risk management is the identification, analysis and treatment of those risks which threaten the viability of the consultant's service. Once a risk has been identified – perhaps a particularly difficult piece of work for a claims conscious client – it can be treated by, on the one hand, simply avoiding that piece of work or, on the other hand, making sure the work gets your very best attention.

Fundamental to a consultant's liability are the terms of the contract with the client, for they govern the rights and liabilities of the contracting parties. Often a contract which should be expressed in clear and unambiguous terms is not. A prudent consultant will spend a great deal of time getting the brief right in the first place. If the help of other consultants is required, their contract should not be open to doubt and they should be adequately insured against their own professional negligence risk. If there are time limits laid down for performing certain parts of the work, these should be clearly documented and adhered to. There should be no room for argument as to the basis of remuneration. Arguments about the fee often produce counterclaims for alleged professional negligence.

Where exclusion or limitation clauses are incorporated into the contract, these must be included before the contract is completed, not added in at a later stage. Most professionals are uneasy about totally excluding their liability for negligence, but are willing to negotiate on limitation – usually calculated as a multiple of the fee charged. Such a limitation, however, only applies as between the parties to a contract. Liability to a third party who suffers loss would not be limited.

One of the most important differences between operating through a company structure and as a sole trader or partnership, besides its management framework and taxation considerations, is professional liability. (Other differences are covered in Chapters 3 and 5.) A company is a distinct legal entity which is separate from its shareholders and directors. A partnership is, on the other hand, the sum of its partners. The liability of members of a limited company (members for this purpose being shareholders) is limited to the extent of their shareholdings. Until fairly recently, incorporation would indeed have been the solution to the professional's liability nightmare. This is not so now, because claims in professional negligence arise in tort as well as in contract and, while such claims both in contract and in tort will be brought against a company as one defendant, an individual employee identified as being responsible for the negligent act will also be joined. For this reason, not only does the company need its own professional indemnity policy, but it must also be one which protects any individual employee.

The cost of professional indemnity insurance is not in any way avoided by incorporation and there is no evidence to suggest that it is reduced. However, there is an essential difference between claims made against an employee of a company and claims made against a partner. First, the company employee must be seen to be personally responsible. Second, personal liability is not joint and several as it would be in a partnership. One director cannot be held personally responsible for a co-director's fault.

Contractual debts are not normally a problem for the professional firm. They are unlikely to enter into contracts that there is no reasonable prospect of meeting, so the undoubted protection that membership of a limited company affords in terms of contractual arrangements is not of prime importance to the professional.

In 1986, the Department of Trade and Industry reviewed professional liability and indemnity insurance and concluded that the only way in which the Government could remove or substantially reduce the professional's risk would be to either 'cap' liability or to provide cover itself, although it did not consider the second option to be feasible. It rejected capping because of its far-reaching implications for both the insurance market and the legal system. It further considered that any ceiling would be arbitrary and, unless the figure was so high as to be irrelevant in most cases, it would have a prejudicial effect on consumers' rights to sue for the full extent of any damage they may have incurred.

Preventing exposure to claims

Most risk management techniques are common sense. They include streamlining office systems, supervising inexperienced staff, making sure you see all incoming and outgoing post and avoiding technical jargon which may be misunderstood by a client. Missing time limits is a prolific source of claims against many consultants. Lawyers fail to issue writs on time, accountants miss completing tax returns, surveyors miss dates for rent reviews, insurance brokers fail to review cover in time, and so on. You should create a system for recording such dates.

Many firms now automatically have on the agenda for management meetings an item covering professional indemnity matters. Emphasis on this relatively new area of concern is bound to grow.

How do consultants become stronger at the service they decide to offer? In recent years, the concept of continuing professional development has gained wide acceptance. The term embodies the UNESCO philosophy of lifelong learning. Most professional organizations now accept that continuing professional development is important for two reasons: it can prevent mistakes and, because it is seen to be happening, the profession is assumed to be exerting a form of quality control over its membership.

More recently, a commitment to continuing professional development has gained a real cutting edge from the suggestion that it should lead to favourable professional indemnity insurance premiums.

Transferring risks to an insurer

The cornerstone of insurance philosophy is the principle of the equitable contribution of many for the benefit of a few individuals suffering loss or loss sharing. However, to make insurance a viable commercial transaction, insurers impose certain limitation on what they will insure. Insurance cover must be arranged within this framework. When risks fall outside the limitations prescribed by the insurer, they become uninsurable.

The strength and capacity of the market for insurance relies, like any market, on information about what is being traded. In the case of professional indemnity insurance, this is a risk. But it is a market in which reliable information is often very hard to find. Those practising professionals who are aware of their shortcomings are likely to take out more insurance than those who are not. Until claims are received, insurers have little way of knowing who is a good or bad risk. The most obvious way to compensate for this is to raise premiums. However, this only drives away the better risks and leaves the bad.

Insurers in the United Kingdom, through the law, have devised another way of dealing with the problem of balancing risks. This is, that contracts of insurance are conducted in the utmost good faith. The prospective insured must declare all relevant information to the insurer. This does not, however, overcome the hazard that the insured, knowing they are covered, will take more risks in their work and behave in a manner unknown to the insurer. The compulsory wearing of seatbelts, it is argued, encourages faster driving. The insurance company then needs not only information about the insured, but also about the way in which they practise their profession. If this alters, the insurance company is left with a policy written on the basis of outdated information.

Such a predicament can lead to insurers offering to cover, or buy, a risk when in fact they are buying a certainty. For a true and healthy market to exist in risk, buyers and sellers need to be sure that the odds are not stacked in favour of one side only. In practice, this probably means maintaining a systems of proving fault as the basis of professional liability.

Reputable brokers have learned not to shop for insurance but to develop long-term relationships with quality insurance companies. But the increasingly litigious environment, the attitude that someone must be sued at all costs, is driving even the well-established insurers from the market. This reduces insurance capacity and brokers find it difficult to find cover of any kind.

The following principles of insurance should apply to an insurable risk:

- it must be a risk that is acceptable to the insurance market through appropriate selection methods;
- it must be fortuitous, that is, accidental in character. As the

probability of a harmful occurrence increases, the premium necessary to cover it increases, too;

- it must be measurable in quantitative terms and in such a way that the theories of probability and the law of the inertia of large numbers may be used;
- it must be such that the cause of any event which results in damages can be determined; and
- the insured must have an insurable interest in the risk which is being insured.

Some twenty years ago, many consultants were not insured against professional indemnity risks. They did not regard the risk of being sued as serious. The insurance market was then in a position of having to 'sell' insurance cover. Now the wheel has turned. Cover is not readily available and what there is, is expensive. Some consultants, then, make the positive decision to practise without professional indemnity cover.

The purpose of professional indemnity insurance is to protect the professional against a legal liability to compensate third parties who have sustained some injury, loss or damage due to negligence on the part of the consultant. Like all liability policies, it is a strictly legal liability contract, not a moral one. Again, like all forms of liability insurance, there is no standard form in use. The following, however, is an example of the sort of cover that is generally available:

> The company agrees subject to the terms exceptions limits and conditions of this policy to indemnify the insured against any claim for damages for breach of professional duty which may be made against him/her during the period of insurance due to any negligent act, error or omission whenever or wherever the same was or was alleged to have been committed by the insured or their predecessors in business or in the conduct of the business.

From this clause, various points emerge:

- The cover relates to claims for damages for breach of professional duty.
- The policy applies to claims made during the period of insurance. Provided the actual claim is made during the period of insurance, it does not matter when the act of negligence giving rise to the claim took place. The policy therefore provides retrospective cover for all acts of negligence committed before inception of the policy. A specific proposal form question, however, will enquire

into this aspect of the risk, and the proposer must be very careful in answering the question as a failure to disclose a potential occurrence which may give rise to a claim in the future could prejudice their cover.

- Cover operates in relation to any negligent act, error or omission. Claims are often reported under policies where the insured may be liable for other reasons, such as dishonesty of staff or contractual warranties or indemnities. These are not covered unless an extension has been negotiated. Actual proof of negligence is not necessary. An allegation of negligence will be within the scope of the policy. The insurers will investigate the allegation and suitably protect the interests of the insured.

- A number of insurers are prepared to issue policies covering claims made against the insured arising out of the civil liability of the insured. The words 'civil liability' are wider than 'negligent act, error or omission' in that they cover liability based on other grounds, for example, breach of contract or breach of warranty regardless of negligence.

- Negligence on the part of the insured, their predecessors in business, and their employees is covered.

The limit of indemnity may be an aggregate limit of indemnity for any one period of insurance, or a limit of indemnity for any one claim, or for any one occurrence. Costs and expenses incurred with the insurer's consent are payable in addition but they are often subject to a form of average. For example, if the limit of indemnity is £200,000 and the claim is settled for £400,000, only 50 per cent of the costs will be paid by the insurer as the insured is only 50 per cent insured.

Territorial limits are not always clear from the policy itself. Most insurers in the United Kingdom intend to cover only work performed in the UK. If work is performed abroad, then this is a material fact which must be disclosed to the insurers.

There are two principal exceptions to most policies. These are libel or slander, and claims brought about or contributed to by the dishonest, fraudulent, criminal or malicious act or omission of the insured, their predecessors in business or employees of the insured or their predecessors in business.

Many consultants find themselves operating in a buyer's market where the client can impose onerous terms on the conditions of engagement. It is not unusual to find the client requiring the consultant to guarantee professional service, or having to indemnify the client against any loss, damage or expense arising out of the performance of the service. Such terms may widen considerably the consultant's liability and should only be accepted after it is ascertained that insurers will cover the additional risk.

A number of practical problems arise if the insured is to obtain the benefit of the policy at the time it is needed. The sad fact is that many insureds fail to get the benefit of their policy because they breach its terms and conditions and this results in the insurer refusing to indemnify them. All policies contain a condition to the effect that the insured cannot, without the written consent of the insurers, repudiate liability for any claim. This is because, as the insurers are going to pay the claim, they reserve for themselves the right to take over and negotiate it. This condition is usually followed by a clause which states that the insured must give the insurers notice in writing immediately of any claim which is made or any intention to hold the consultant responsible for breach of professional duty. Both these conditions can be difficult for the insured to comply with in practice. Moreover, many policies provide that if, during the policy, the insured becomes aware of any 'occurrence' which may give rise to a claim, then it must be notified. The difficulty is in recognizing an occurrence which should be notified. One advantage to the insured is that, once the occurrence has been notified, the insurers will deal with any subsequent claim arising from it, even though the policy may have lapsed. In other words, the claim, even when made many years later, is attached to the policy in force when the occurrence was reported.

An insurance broker can help in the identification and management of risks, including the extremely important process of applying for cover, and representing your insurance needs to an underwriter. A consultant should exercise the same care in selecting an insurance broker as he or she would in selecting a solicitor. A good broker will help in the following ways:

- evaluate your liability exposure and make you aware of various forms of insurance;
- communicate with the insurance market;
- apply particular criteria in evaluating and recommending a specific insurance programme;

- give advice on insurance implications of the changes in the organizational structure or the nature of your work;
- review proposed contractual provisions affecting insurability;
- develop a management programme for you; and
- monitor claims.

Just as a project belongs to a client, the consultant 'owns' an insurance policy and must make all the final decisions. The broker's obligation is to make certain these decisions are as informed as possible.

References

Buzzell, R. D. et al. (1975), 'Market share: a key to profitability', in *Harvard Business Review*, January/February.

Garratt, R. (1981), *From Expertise to Contingency: Changes in the Nature of Consultancy*, Management Education and Development (Workshop), Vol. 12, pt. 2, pp 95–101.

Garratt, S. (1985 and 1990), *Manage Your Time*, Fontana.

GMS Consultancy (1990) *The Independent Consultancy Market*, reported by Michael Dixon in the *Financial Times*, 4 April. (Available from GMS Consultancy, 48 High Street North, Dunstable, Bedfordshire LU6 1LA   Tel: 0582 666970.)

Holtz, H. (1988), *How to Succeed as an Independent Consultant*, Wiley.

Revans, R. (1982), *The Origins of Action Learning*, Chartwell-Bratt.

Recommended Reading

Bentley, Trevor J. (1987), *Report Writing in Business*, Kogan Page.
Bone, Diane (1988), *A Practical Guide to Effective Listening*, Kogan Page.
Bryson, Bill (1987), *Dictionary of Troublesome Words*, Penguin.
Bunch, Meribeth (1989), *Speak with Confidence*, Kogan Page.
Buzan, Tony (1987), *Use Your Head*, BBC Publications.
Cooper, Bruce M. (1987), *Writing Technical Reports*, Penguin.
Fletcher, J. A. and D. F. Gowing (1987), *The Business Guide to Effective Writing*, Kogan Page.
Garratt, Sally (1986, 1990), *Manage Your Time*, Fontana.
Haynes, Marion E. (1988), *Effective Meeting Skills*, Kogan Page.
Horn, Sandra (1986), *Relaxation*, Thorsons.
Lloyd, Sam R. (1988), *How to Develop Assertiveness*, Kogan Page.
Mandel, Steve (1987), *Effective Presentation Skills*, Kogan Page.
Moncrieff, Joan and Doreen Sharp (1986), *The PA's Handbook*, Papermac.
Pythian, B. A. (comp.) (1989), *A Concise Dictionary of Correct English*, Hodder & Stoughton.
Ramage, Philippa (1986), *Be a Successful Secretary*, Pitman.
Roman, Eva (1983), *The Office Partnership*, Video Arts Limited.
Stanton, Nicki (1986), *The Business of Communicating*, Pan.
Stanton, Nicki (1986), *What Do You Mean 'Communcation'?*, Pan.
Wright, Christine (1988), *Report Writing*, Industrial Society.

Index